ZONDERVAN.com/
AUTHORTRACKER
follow your favorite authors

Youth Specialties products, 300 South Pierce Street, El Cajon, CA 92020, are published by Zondervan, 5300 Patterson Avenue Southeast, Grand Rapids, MI 49530.

Library of Congress Cataloging-in-Publication Data

Losey, John, 1965-
Experiential youth ministry handbook : how intentional activity can make the spiritual stuff stick / by John Losey.
p. cm.
Includes bibliographical references.
ISBN-10: 0-310-27096-0 (pbk.)
ISBN-13: 978-0-310-27096-6 (pbk.)
1. Church work with youth. I. Title.
BV4447 .L66 2004
259'.23—dc22

2003025493

Web site addresses listed in this book were current at the time of publication. Please contact Youth Specialties via e-mail (YS@YouthSpecialties.com) to report URLs that are no longer operational and provide replacement URLs if available.

Creative Team: Dave Urbanski, Laura Gross, Heather Haggerty, Rich Cairnes, and David Conn
Cover design by Toolbox Studios
Printed in the United States

08 09 10 11 12 • 23 22 21 20 19 18 17 16 15 14 13 12 11 10 9 8 7 6 5 4 3 2

DEDICATION

This book is dedicated to:

Russ Rogers, who taught me that thinking clearly is as fun as playing freely.

Dave Hopkins, who taught me that a thankful spirit is possible in all things and is much more satisfying than a critical spirit.

Priscilla Losey, my amazing wife who is teaching me daily about love and generosity.

CONTENTS

INTRODUCTION

Experience has always been the best teacher

Early in my career working with students, I learned that leading group prayer is a lot like learning to climb rocks.[1] My best friend Tommy and I were just starting our sophomore year in college and volunteering for Campus Life high school ministry. The big kickoff for the year was when we invited the whole high school to an all-you-can-eat pizza and root beer party. The students paid 50 cents to get access to the food, and they stayed for a slide show[2] and invitation to check out the weekly club meetings that would take place the rest of the year.

[1] Really it is. Just stick with me on this one.

[2] Slide shows using two projectors and a dissolve unit were the height of technology at that time.

One of Tommy's responsibilities for the evening was leading prayer before the meal. He and I had grown up in the church together, and we had prayed in front of people many times. This was a bit different. There were more than 400 students there—but few of them made a habit of praying before a meal. The energy in the room was high, and the smell of hot pizza made the students even more restless.

Tommy stood on stage and said into the microphone, "Okay, we're gonna pray for the food now."

The students continued to talk and look around the room as they waited for the pizza to appear.

Tommy tried again, "Hey, you guys quiet down so we can pray."

Few, if any, students noticed him standing on the stage.

"Be quiet so I can pray!"

Still no change in the sound level.

"OKAY YOU GUYS! I'M NOT GOING TO PRAY UNTIL IT'S TOTALLY QUIET IN HERE!" Now Tommy's frustration was apparent to everyone in the room. Still, no one paid any attention to him, and it seemed he'd never begin his prayer.

At this point, our more experienced director, Ken, said, "Just start praying."

"What?" replied Tommy.

"Just start praying, and they'll settle down."

Tommy looked back at Ken with skepticism, then turned to the microphone and began to pray, "Dear God, thank you for—" Before he could finish the first sentence, the room had quieted down; and while not all of the students were praying, Tommy[3] had their attention.

[3] Tommy is now an ordained Presbyterian minister and a very talented preacher and teacher. He's also still one of my best friends.

When learning how to rock climb, you often hear an instructor or more experienced partner say "lean back and trust your feet." To the novice hanging desperately from the smooth face of a huge slab of rock, this seems insane. Your feet slip and slide while you try to morph your body to the rock and hold most of your weight by the tips of your fingers. Why would you trust your unstable footing? Why would you move your body ***away*** from the rock?

What the more experienced climber knows is that your feet are slipping because you don't trust them. She knows that as you move your body away from the rock, your feet will get more friction and hold more firmly to the rock. When climbing, the only way to learn to trust your feet is to actually ***trust*** your feet and experience the stability. It's by actually moving your body away from the rock that you learn how much easier climbing can be.

Through Tommy's experience, we both learned a valuable and practical lesson in ministry: ***If you wait until everything is under control before you start, you may never start.*** This is true for leading prayer for a group of students, as well as for much of life. "Just start praying" makes as little sense as "Lean back and trust your feet." That is, until you try it.[4] Once you've experienced them, these types of life lessons can be used over and over again. We learn skills such as public speaking or rock climbing best through experience, but we can also use our experience to move concepts from abstract ideas to transformational encounters.

[4] See footnote 1. See, I told you they'd connect!

Did you know that experience transforms both math[5] and faith into life? "Why do I have to take math? I'll never use this in real life." You hear this plea of frustration from students trapped in a classroom doing page after page of equations.[6] They have yet to connect ***x*** to anything remotely connected to life. But when ***x*** becomes a batting average, a discount on clothes, or how they can get enough money for the latest video game, they begin to see how algebra can change their lives and why they should spend a little time doing their homework. We all "do math" every day, but we seldom notice it. Given real consequences, math becomes real life.

[5] "Math? You said there would be no math." —Chevy Chase as President Ford (*Saturday Night Live*, c. 1975)

[6] I feared math throughout high school and well into college. I know of what I speak.

Faith—along with grace, service, and other key concepts of a life following Christ—can remain distant and abstract until they burst into life through experience. It's not that we don't experience these things every day; on the contrary, we constantly encounter God's love, mercy, and grace! We just don't notice it. Just as we "do math" every day but seldom call it "math," we witness God's work on a daily basis but seldom see it.[7]

[7] *Witness* versus *see*. Just because you're present when something happens—or even if you notice an event as it occurs—that doesn't mean you really see it. My intention is to stress the importance of connecting experience and meaning.

In the same way, we can use the common experiences from our students' day-to-day lives and create experiences to help them notice what and where God wants them to grow—on both an individual and group level. We can help individuals understand themselves, and how they can be more effective in all areas of their lives; we can help groups intentionally develop a flourishing community that accomplishes great things while still taking care of its people. The intentional use of experience creates an environment that encourages the continual growth of students and adult staff.

Helping Students Unwrap Their Gifts

My brother's family has a strong tradition surrounding Christmas. There are different jobs that must be done each year.[8] The most prestigious and sought-after position is that of "Santa" or the one who passes out the gifts. This person's job is to read the gift tags and make sure the gifts get into the right hands. And if a gift is missing a tag, then Santa must match the gift with the unattached tags left under the tree.

[8] These jobs include putting out the cookies and milk, being the "scout" or the first one to see the presents, and the coveted "Santa" position.

Similarly, we often need a "Santa" to reveal to us the life lessons wrapped inside our own experiences. While we're always experiencing life, we seldom take advantage of the lessons that are available to us through these experiences. They're like wonderfully wrapped gifts that remain unopened under the Christmas tree. Many are unlabeled and just require someone to point and say, "That's yours. Open it up and try it out." We're at our best as leaders, teachers, and pastors when we help people notice these unopened gifts by pointing to them and inviting students to open them up and play with them. This is using experience on purpose to transform lives.

Noticing, pointing, inviting, and playing[9] may seem like simple skills, but they must be taught and practiced. We're not trained to lead and teach in this way. This presents a major hurdle for us before we can be intentional about experiential methods in our work and lives. Many of us started our ministry experiences as volunteers with little, if any, training. We raised our hands or signed an "interest sheet"[10] and suddenly we found ourselves in front of a group of kids with a "talk sheet" in our hands. In that moment our desire for thorough, authentic training took a nosedive when compared to our desire to survive the encounter with the students.[11] Some of us may have entered ministry after many years of higher education or seminary. Fully loaded with theology and theory, we walked into our first encounter with students wishing we knew more about how to just get and hold their attention.

[9] Noticing, pointing, inviting, and playing are the four primary roles we play when we take advantage of experiential methods.

[10] Curiosity can be misinterpreted as commitment, especially by stressed-out youth pastors who are short on volunteers.

[11] "Just tell me what to do!" becomes the desperate cry of new or undertrained youth workers.

Our current practice of training leaders and teachers focuses either on tips, tricks, and techniques, or on theory and models. Usually one is given priority over the other, or they're sequenced so one must precede the other.

"The Rabbit of Seville" Philosophy of Education

However, that great learning theorist—Bugs Bunny[12]—points us to another training approach. In the "Rabbit of Seville" episode (Warner Bros., 1950), Bugs and Elmer Fudd demonstrate a simple form of praxis[13] as a way of growth. We find both Bugs and Elmer sitting in barber chairs. Both have handles that let them ratchet up their chairs higher. Bugs—representing the practical and pragmatic—ratchets himself up just a bit higher than Elmer; Mr. Fudd—representing the theoretical and philosophical[14]—works the handle on his chair back and forth until he reaches Bugs' chair. Bugs, feeling threatened by the unreality of theory, brings his chair once again much higher than Fudd's. Elmer responds to the resulting imbalance by positioning his chair near the same height as Bugs'. This process of adjustment and repositioning continues until both barber chairs reach far up into the heavens. Both Bugs (practical/pragmatic) and Elmer (theoretical/philosophical) find themselves developed higher and farther than if they were separate from each other. The "Rabbit

[12] Okay, so Bugs isn't up there with Piaget, Dewey, or Lewen. But if we stretch our imaginations, this example works.

[13] While the Bugs Bunny Theory (focus on theory to action) may match some popular definitions of praxis, it lacks the reflection component that I believe is essential to the concept of praxis. (See my first *Experiential Youth Ministry Handbook* (YS/Zondervan, 2004).)

[14] Bugs as pragmatic and Elmer as theoretical are arbitrary distinctions. If you get hung up on the symbolism of the characters, feel free to reverse the connection.

of Seville" philosophy of education translates easily into how we can design and implement training for our staff, our students, and ourselves.

Translation: ***Action (practical/pragmatic—Bugs) and Theory (theoretical/ philosophical—Elmer) are essential and equal in importance to teaching, leading, and transforming people.***[15]

[15] Again, let me stress that this "translation," while true to the Bugs Bunny model, lacks the reflection aspect of praxis (defined as the interpenetration of action, reflection, and theory).

I discuss praxis further in the first ***Experiential Youth Ministry Handbook.*** (That book also explores the "Learning Loop of Depth"—the cyclical nature of experience in teaching.) The first volume leans heavily toward the intentional use of experience from a programming perspective, while this book you're reading now looks at experiential methods from a slightly different angle. If my first book is about planning, programming, and events, then this one looks at the role experience plays in learning, development, and growth.

Why This Book Was Written

Simply to encourage teachers and leaders to use experience on purpose to help students grow. While you encounter the observations in this book, you'll become a better **observer**. As you notice new or different ideas about teaching and leading, you can begin to **point to** the lessons available to the people you teach and lead. This book invites you to new perspectives about ministry and how it might be lived. Therefore, you're encouraged to **invite** others to live the lessons to which you're pointing. You may need to claim an environment where you can try out these new concepts and skills—i.e., a place for your students and staff where they feel safe to **play**.

This book contains **models and theories** (Elmer Fudd stuff). It also contains **activities and exercises** (Bugs Bunny stuff). The last section of this book offers **templates** or common situations where these models can meet these activities in real life. You're invited to observe what these theories look like in real life and how these activities can be used on purpose.

How to Get the Most Out of *EYMH2*

Read this book experientially. Have you noticed the **margin notes**?[16] They're not there just to cite sources or point you to further reading and information. I've added them to give you a glimpse into the dialog I have with this material. They're an invitation to join the conversation and interact with the material.

I also recommend that you **read with a pen.**[17] As you join the conversation surrounding this book, write down any comments, questions, and thoughts in the margins. Don't just highlight or underline the text; be sure to write ***why*** you underlined or highlighted it. And include the stuff you don't like right along with the stuff you do.[18]

Don't stop at reading experientially. My hope is that you'll also **try this stuff.** But don't try all of it at the same time. There is more in this book than what you can live right away.[19] Do the stuff with which you connect. Do the stuff you can do and

[16] I hope so.

[17] This is good advice for any reading you do. I'm amazed by the deep and practical insights that assault me as I read even the most trivial drivel.

[18] It's usually the stuff that I hate or have the strongest reaction to that has the most significance for me. Ask why it's impacting you so much. It might have more to do with you than with the material.

[19] The point is to live it out, not just read it or "know" it. See Rainer Maria Rilke's *Letters to a Young Poet* (New World Library, 2000).

want to do. Don't do it just because you think you should. Your passion will carry you higher and deeper into effectiveness.

Know that attempting something once isn't really trying it. My friend Tom Leahy gives his Theory of Threes as a way of knowing when you've really tried something: The first time you attempt something, you really don't know what you're doing; the second attempt creates some clarity of what you're really going to try; the third attempt is the first time you can really evaluate whether or not an idea or method works. So when you live this stuff out, be sure to attempt something at least three times before you deem it a failure (or success).

Last Words of Advice

- Dive into what you love.
- Attempt what scares you.
- File away what seems irrelevant now.
- Rewrite or reinvent the things that don't make sense or seem stupid.
- Find the joy and humor in everything you attempt.
- Enjoy the adventure!

Section One

FOUNDATIONS

STAGES OF GROWTH

Chapter 1.1

"It's the fundamentals, boys." —Vince Lombardi

I was a champion wrestler in high school. Looking at me today, you might think that amazing.[20] What's even more amazing is that I didn't really want to go to the championship tournament. My loyalty to Coach Pry was the only reason I'd joined the team in the first place. I'd wrestled since junior high, and I enjoyed the sport; but I'd also hurt my knee the previous two years. Now in my senior year, I was looking forward to playing football in college, and I didn't want to do further damage to my knee. Word got around to Coach Pry that I was considering not participating that season, and he approached me.

"John," he said, "I hear you might not wrestle this year. Without you we only have a sophomore to wrestle heavyweight. You're a bit light for that weight class,[21] but I think you could do well. What do you think?"

He hooked me with two things: My loyalty and my desire for challenge. So I joined the team.

Every season started the same way. No matter how long you'd been wrestling, you had to start from the basics: The sprawl and the drop step. We drilled these moves at the start of every practice, and the experienced wrestlers did these drills right alongside the beginners. Later in the practice session we'd be allowed to drill more advanced moves, but not until we'd practiced the basics. Every single day.

As the new wrestlers became more comfortable with the basic moves, Coach Pry would stop the drill and gather everyone around him. He'd then demonstrate a complete move broken down into component steps: 1) drop step, 2) head on the outside, 3) wrap arms around both legs, 4) suck the legs in with your arms and pull your hips under you, and 5) complete your drop step while turning and lifting the opponent off the mat.[22] We'd begin to drill this move one step at a time, moving to step three only after we could smoothly combine steps one and two. Coach Pry would count off, "1, 2, 3, 4, 5. Switch partners. 1, 2, 3, 4, 5...," and he'd increase the tempo as we became more comfortable with the move. He'd have us practice a few times without counting, and then he'd turn us loose to spar at full speed.

[20] When I look in the mirror each morning, I'm shocked at what's left of a once athletic body.

[21] "You're a bit light for that weight class." Again, times have changed.

[22] Now you know how to do a "double leg takedown." Try it on a friend.

By the end of that section of practice, all of us—both the experienced and the "newbies"—had a complete understanding of the move and knew how to use it in real wrestling situations. Coach Pry introduced two or three new moves a week this way. Because of his approach, our team won our league and sent eight guys to the finals of the league tournament.

I learned much from Coach Pry that year, but I learned far more from him when I worked as one of his assistant coaches. The year after I graduated from high school, he accepted a teaching and coaching job 20 minutes from where I was going to college. My football career went by the wayside, and I ended up volunteering for Campus Life at the same high school where he was working. As a way to be on campus, I helped him coach freshman football and wrestling.

I wanted to show the students all that I knew as a football player and wrestler, but my approach frustrated both the students and me. First, I'd show them what I believed to be a simple blocking technique—and they'd give me a puzzled look and trip over their own feet as they tried to copy the move.

Finally, Coach Pry pulled me aside and said, "They need to learn how to get ***into*** a basic stance before they can learn how to get out of it. Don't start with the whole thing; start with the basics and then build on them." This made a whole lot of sense, and it still impacts how I plan my programs and curricula.

Steps and Stages

Breaking down a concept into component parts and introducing students to these parts one at a time while building on the previous concept is one way of understanding how steps and stages of learning can help us be more effective teachers, coaches, and leaders. Just as it's important to understand what we're teaching, we must also understand how much students can handle, and how they learn and grow.

This section offers some simple imagery that might help us become more intentional in helping people grasp new concepts and move through difficult stages in life.

From Milk to Meat—Sequenced Learning

When Coach Pry introduced us to the basic skills first and then added progressively more complex aspects of wrestling, he was modeling a sequenced approach to learning. By first offering easy, accessible skills, he not only built a foundation for what was to come, but he also allowed us to experience success and created fun and excitement.

The Bible talks about this process as a movement from milk to meat.

> You've had a taste of God. Now, like infants at the breast, drink deep of God's pure kindness. Then you'll grow up mature and whole in God.—1 Peter 2:2-3 (*The Message*)

> Brothers, I could not address you as spiritual but as worldly—mere infants in Christ. I gave you milk, not solid food, for you were not yet ready for it. Indeed, you are still not ready.—1 Corinthians 3:1-2

We start as infants, immature and limited in our capacity to digest. In order to survive, we must be fed simple things that we can easily process. Just as this is true for newborns to grow, it's also true when we're like "newborns" to unfamiliar ideas, concepts, and skills. Babies' systems cannot handle solid, complex food. They cannot chew it, and their stomachs can't digest it. In fact, their bodies will reject the food, and it will make them sick.

Similarly, if we offer advanced and complex concepts or skills to students who aren't yet advanced enough to properly "digest" them, then we risk doing damage. We need to distill the lesson down to the foundational elements and create "bite-sized" chunks that match the learner's ability to digest and apply. These chunks can then be arranged so one builds onto the next.[23]

[23] Like the double leg takedown, ideas and concepts can be distilled to component concepts that build on each other and increase in complexity and sophistication.

> We have much to say about this, but it is hard to explain because you are slow to learn. In fact, though by this time you ought to be teachers, you need someone to teach you the elementary truths of God's word all over again. You need milk, not solid food! Anyone who lives on milk, being still an infant, is not acquainted with the teaching about righteousness. But solid food is for the mature, who by constant use have trained themselves to distinguish good from evil. Therefore let us leave the elementary teachings about Christ and go on to maturity, not laying again the foundation of repentance from acts that lead to death, and of faith in God. —Hebrews 5:11–6:1

As an infant matures, she needs more than just milk for continued growth. Her body needs more complex food in order to meet the demands of a growing body. The author of Hebrews knows this. He challenges the readers of his letter to move on to solid food so they can become mature. As we teach and lead, we need to pay attention to the people we work with. We need to be ready to offer increasingly more "solid food" as they become ready to digest it and to ask them to deal with increasingly complex ideas and skills so they're encouraged to continue to mature.[24]

[24] The implication of this is that we leaders need to continue to challenge ourselves to increased complexity. We need to find sources for our meat.

Soap Box[25]—Different Flavors of Milk

[25] This section is a "soap box" because it's infused with my opinions and bias, and my passion may have impacted the presentation.

Moving from milk to meat isn't easy. It's a challenge—not only for the learner, but for the teacher as well. Too often we, as teachers, don't rise to this challenge. Instead of pressing on to more complex and demanding levels, we just change the flavor of the milk. We grab the Nesquik and make chocolate milk. Content with offering a simplistic understanding, we just move on to another topic. It may taste different, but it's still milk.

Once the basics of this new topic are covered, again the leader is faced with the choice of going deeper and demanding more growth (offering meat) or moving on to a different topic (finding a new flavor of milk). Flavored milk is fine for infants, but it can't sustain growth. There comes a point where a diet of milk actually stunts growth rather than encouraging it.

Mules, Canyon Willow, and the Illusion of Growth

During the gold rush days of the 1850s, miners were astonished to find their fat mules dying of starvation. The men who panned for gold spent most of their time camped beside creeks and streams. They allowed their animals to feed freely on whatever plants they found nearby. The mules were attracted to Canyon Willow, a plant with green, juicy leaves that were easy to reach. The animals would gorge themselves on these leaves until they were plump and appeared well fed.[26] However, when the miners put their packs on the mules and prompted them to work, they found the usually energetic but stubborn animals seemed tired, lethargic, and unable to carry even the lightest workload. The mules looked fat, but they were actually starving to death.

[26] The miners started to call Canyon Willow "Mule Fat."

As it turns out, the Canyon Willow leaves contain lots of water but almost no nutrients. So the mules would eat these nutritiously empty but easily accessible plants until they were stuffed. Then they had no desire to eat anything else. They looked fat and happy; but they weren't getting the vitamins, minerals, protein, or any other important nutrients they needed to sustain life. Thus the mules would die fat.

We face the same temptation as those mules. The milk—the simple concepts so easily accessed—won't provide the nutrients or the meat of diving deeper into those concepts that we need to grow and to survive. Are we allowing the people we're supposed to be leading and teaching to graze on Mule Fat? Are we helping people grow fat while they're essentially starving to death?

Chew Your Food (Ruminate)—Meditation

"Chew your food!" I can still hear my mom's voice ringing in my ears as I gulped down a meal. As a child I didn't like eating meat. You had to chew it too much. I just wanted food you could shove in your mouth, chomp down once or twice, and then swallow. This method works great for soft foods such as yogurt and oatmeal, but not so well on a nice steak.[27] Chewing takes big chunks of food and breaks them into pieces that, first, fit into your throat, and second, are most effectively digested and absorbed by your system.

[27] In high school I choked on an unchewed piece of steak. If not for the Heimlich maneuver, I would have died (or at least been extremely inconvenienced).

Meditation finds its roots in the same concept as a cow chewing its cud.[28] A cow chews its food several times so it can get every last bit of the nutrients and energy from the difficult-to-digest grass on which it feeds. It actively grazes, and then it finds a quiet place to hang out and chew. To look at a cow chewing its cud, you wouldn't think much is going on. It's just sitting there. No real action. But the cow could never survive without this "passive' activity. Meditation requires this same type of essential nonaction. The cow offers a great example of how we can meditate and create opportunities for growth for those we teach and lead.

[28] Much thanks to Rick Hicks for the connection between meditation and cows.

Meditation first requires some good stuff to chew on. If a cow is chewing on Mule Fat,[29] then it doesn't matter how ***much*** it chews—it's going to starve. The

[29] See footnote on Canyon Willow. It has few nutrients to start with so you can't get any more from continual chewing.

cow has to have good grass in order to get what its body needs. In the same way, meditation is only as powerful as that on which you meditate. It starts with a rich text, lesson, or experience.

Now this next part may seem silly, but some people need permission to meditate. They may not know how vital it is, or they may associate meditation with strange workshops on Eastern mysticism. However, this concept of meditation[30] was quite common to first-century people, and it's found throughout the Bible. So not only do you have permission to meditate, but you're also encouraged to do so. As a teacher and leader, you need to give that same permission and encouragement to your students.

[30] Meditation as in repeatedly chewing the content or information for a more complete understanding.

While cows don't need much permission or encouragement to chew, they do need a place and the time to do it. We also need to find or create a place and clear out a section of our schedules for meditation. However, "inaction" isn't highly valued today. We cram our schedules full of very urgent and "valuable" things[31] but seldom do we take the time to let these experiences and lessons impact and improve our lives. T. S. Eliot said, "We had the experience but missed the meaning." Too often we experience a meaty lesson or a powerful experience and move on without really considering all it might hold for us. However, meditation allows us to squeeze as much content and meaning from each lesson as possible. This can only happen if we give ourselves a chance to chew—to open up a time and place for meditation.

[31] Or with totally worthless but very entertaining things, such as *Judge Judy* or PlayStation.

Seasons of Life—Steps, Spirals, and Pyramids

By breaking content into bite-sized chunks and sequencing our presentation, we can encourage deeper and more powerful learning. Beyond looking at the **content** we intend to present as "chunks," we can also increase the power of our teaching and leading by looking at the ways **people** learn and develop as being a series of steps or stages, as well as different seasons, each with its own unique set of issues and challenges.

The disciple John points out the unique roles we play at different stages of our lives,[32] suggesting that we have different purposes depending on our age or maturity. The third chapter of Ecclesiastes suggests there are seasons for everything and a proper time for every purpose under heaven. The Bible not only acknowledges there are steps and stages in development, but also it suggests that we offer leadership and teaching based on an understanding of what's appropriate at each stage.[33] By gaining a better understanding of the sequences and seasons of learning and their unique challenges, we can intentionally create opportunities that encourage students to continued growth.

[32] 1 John.

[33] New wine in old wineskins.

So what do I mean by "seasons" or by a "sequence" of learning and development? While working on a master's degree in social science, I was introduced to several models in developmental psychology and learning theory. In the midst of the intricacy and complexity of these models, I noticed some commonalities. Most of these theories use a simple picture or concept to help explain people's journey of development. These simple pictures offered me useful insights into how to structure learning situations, even before I grasped the subtle nuances of the complete theories.

Let me offer four simplified models of how people learn and develop.[34] These basic structures of developmental theory can be starting points for being intentional in how you create stand-alone events or more long-term programs.

[34] These models have been distilled from much more precise and specific studies in developmental psychology (cognitive, psychosocial and moral/faith development) and education.

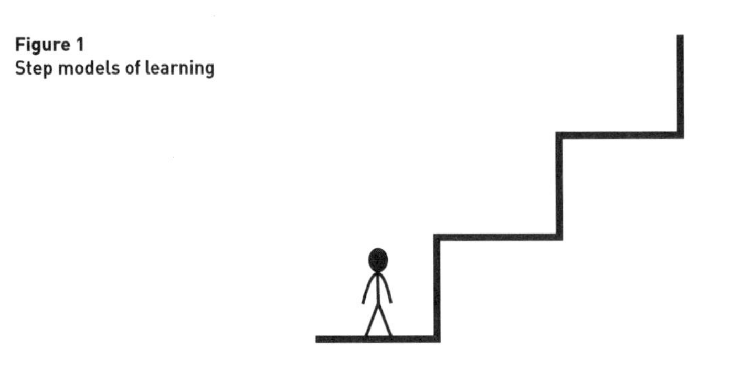
Figure 1
Step models of learning

Steps

Picture a staircase, a series of steps leading to a different level. You stand at the base of one of the steps, just looking at the sharp incline and knowing it'll take energy and effort to take that next step up. This is the most basic, common picture used in understanding learning and growth. We stand on the horizontal step facing a vertical rise. Where we're standing and the steps we've already taken represent our knowledge, abilities, and perspectives. The vertical rise represents the challenge we're facing—a new situation for which our lives to date haven't prepared us. Now we must gain new experiences, skills, or insights before we can attempt the next step. It may take several attempts, but this step must be addressed before any others can be attempted.

This step picture of development (figure 1) has been applied to major issues such as self versus other, identity, and to more specific issues such as concrete versus abstract thinking. Whatever the issue or topic, viewing **learning as a series of steps** that needs to be addressed and surmounted can give us some useful insight into how to design learning opportunities. A bit of further study on these specific steps or challenges can help you be even more intentional in predicting challenges and helping people take their next steps forward.

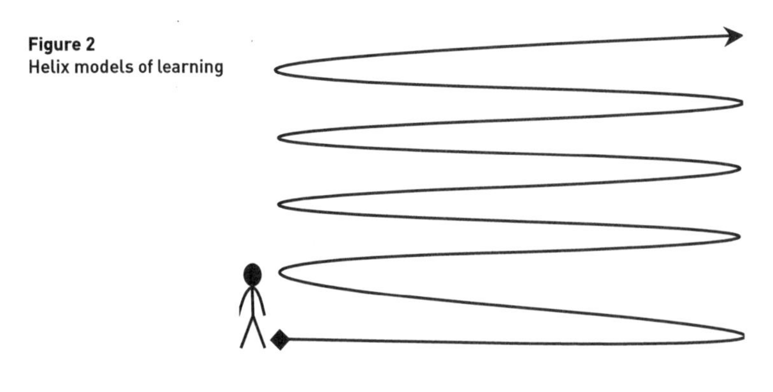
Figure 2
Helix models of learning

Helix[35]

[35] A fancy name for a spiral.

As we live and learn, we often notice themes in our lives—topics of learning we seem to relive over and over, but at different levels of complexity. The picture of a helix or a spiral can be helpful in understanding this model of development (figure 2). Whether you picture the spiral going up (dealing with issues at a higher level) or going down (addressing challenges in a deeper way), the helix offers a new perspective. For instance, people may find themselves challenged by topics they've addressed in their pasts. This can be frustrating until they understand that while the issues may be similar, now they're in new places and have new skills and experiences to deal with these issues. Therefore they're more likely to face this new challenge and squeeze more learning and growth from the experiences.

The parables do this to and for me. I grew up going to Sunday school and hearing the parables taught over and over again.[36] I've been learning from them for 40 years. Yet I'm amazed each time I learn something new from one of them. My life experiences and continued learning combine with Jesus' amazing insight and storytelling to present content that I'd never noticed until that moment.

[36] I can still picture the flannelgraph Jesus pointing to the different pictures of sheep and goats.

The picture of a helix can also help you anticipate resistance to common topics and encourage people to continue to learn and grow from the everyday aspects of their lives.

Figure 3
Pyramid models of learning

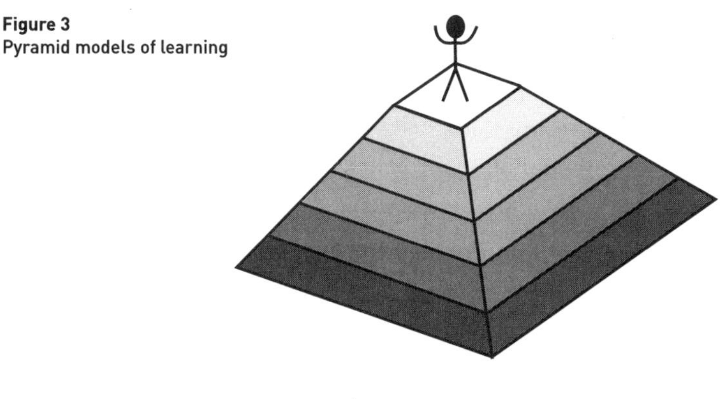

Pyramids

Some developmental issues cannot be addressed until a foundation is created through the successful resolution of ***other*** issues. A pyramid (figure 3) creates a helpful picture of this process. A broad, stable foundational layer is created. Once this ground level has been constructed, another smaller layer can be added. This model stresses the importance of fundamentals in the continued growth and development of people. As a teacher, you must attend to your students' basic needs; they won't notice your wonderful illustrations or the powerful object lessons you offer if they're hungry, cold, or in fear for their lives.[37] As you attend to fundamental needs, you'll be able to address more complex issues.

[37] I've missed some valuable lessons because I overslept.

Knowing a student's ability or skill level can also offer a useful foundation on which to build. Coach Pry pointed that out to me. It was no use teaching football players how to block until I'd built the foundational skills of getting into and out of a good stance. Understanding the needs and skill levels of your teenagers, how these needs and skills are applied and addressed, and how they interact can help you know when to challenge people to grow and when to offer support so they can heal and move forward.

Explosive Encounters—Transforming Moments

One last picture of growth and development doesn't fit into step or stage models—because quantum learning can happen in an explosive instant. For instance, losing a loved one or winning the lottery rocks what you know of the world; these kinds of transforming moments change your worldview at the very core of who you are. All of your life experiences and all the coping skills you've acquired to that point no longer help you understand your world. In the blink of an eye, you discover that you need to find new ways to comprehend your life.

Saul's experience on the road to Damascus is one such encounter. When he's confronted by Jesus, whose followers he's been persecuting, Saul's world is forever changed. He spends time with Barnabas and learns the basics of his new life. As leaders and teachers, we may also encounter students who've experienced a transforming moment—either through tragedy or triumph. Being able to recognize the need for a total reconstruction of how they see the world will be essential to helping them take their next steps forward. We can never predict when we'll encounter this type of radical growth, but we can be ready to respond when it does happen.

Implications and Applications

I remember meeting a fifth-grader at summer camp. His parents were in the beginning stages of what would turn into a nasty divorce. He hurt as he learned that his parents would do anything to him and through him to get back at each other. He blamed himself as he learned that his value was determined by the gifts with which his parents used to bribe him. He was a sweet kid, but he was learning to survive in his world by manipulation.

I met this same kid in high school—not the exact ***same*** kid, mind you, but a student who had lived through a similar history. He was obnoxious and difficult to be around. He gained attention through harsh words and a tough attitude—the results of having to survive in a tough family.

So keep these truths in mind:

- Knowing where people come from and what they've been through is essential to knowing how to teach and lead them.
- Knowing the steps and stages people have gone through—whether it's their specific histories or just general theories of development—can make it possible to love those people more effectively.
- Knowing stage models of learning and growth can offer insights into people's situations; if you know where they're at, you can meet them there.
- You can offer them challenges that will stretch them but are still within their grasps.
- Stage models can also offer insight into what may be waiting for people down the road—and therefore you can offer lessons and learning opportunities that will build the skills and insights that'll help them better navigate the journey.

DYNAMICS OF GROWTH

Chapter 1.2

Let's get the bad news out of the way first. Growth and development begin to happen only when we're uncomfortable.[38] And, usually, the more uncomfortable we are, the greater the growth. I learned to tie my shoes as a child because I got impatient waiting for my mother (or some other more advanced person[39]) to do it for me. A mild inconvenience, but it motivated me to learn a basic task.

[38] When I say things like this, some say I have the gift of discouragement.

[39] My father, other adults, or even my brothers would qualify as a "more advanced person."

A few years later, I learned a much more painful and more valuable lesson. I had a friend in sixth grade named James. He had a paper route, and once he asked me to deliver the papers while he went out of town with his family. It wasn't a ***real*** newspaper. It was delivered free to all the houses in the area, and it contained a bunch of advertisements, coupons, and a few articles.[40] The day came for me to pick up, fold, and deliver the papers to the driveways and porches of the neighborhood. I picked up the 75 copies and folded all of them into neat little rolls. Then I began to think about riding my bike up and down the hills and carrying all those papers. It's at that moment that stupidity seemed to seize my brain.

[40] I believe the coupons were the source of my miscalculation.

The re-creation of my thought process follows:

1. This is a whole lot of papers.
2. There are several fairly steep hills along the route.
3. This is going to be very difficult.
4. People don't have to pay for the paper, so they don't really want it.
5. They won't miss it if it's not delivered.
6. If I dump all the papers in the fields, nobody will know and nobody will miss getting the paper.

Then I followed this flawed thought process right into the undeveloped fields near my house and dumped the papers.

The results were far from what I expected. Apparently, there were people who ***used*** those coupons. After they called and complained about not receiving the paper,[41] not only did I not get paid for the job, but I also had to pay $37.50 to the publishers to make up for the missing papers. Then James was fired from the paper route, and he stopped being my friend.

[41] I've since learned how important coupons can be to some people.

Paying back the $37.50, which was a huge sum for a sixth-grader back then, was painful; losing James as a friend was devastating. The pain of these poor choices taught me the importance of integrity and offered me an opportunity to think about what it means when a friend trusts you, and you let him down. This self-inflicted discomfort was intense for a kid, but the lessons I learned were deep and powerful. I gained life skills that I'd lacked up to that point, and the consequences of my actions opened my eyes to my own need.

Discomfort is typically the result after we encounter a situation for which we're not equipped or prepared. Whether this result is because of our own poor choices or because of situations out of our control, pain and discomfort show us where we're lacking. They also encourage us to find new skills, tools, or perspectives to help us deal with the situation better.

The Bible and Discomfort

God seems to understand the role that discomfort plays in our growth.[42] James, the leader of the church in Jerusalem, was no stranger to pain. Being followers of Jesus and being surrounded by the people who killed Jesus, James and the people in his church are targets for abuse and bad treatment. They live with the very real threat of bodily harm and death every day. James labels this kind of pain and discomfort as "trials" and encourages us not only to accept them, but also to "consider it pure joy" when we go through them.

[42] Hmm...perhaps because he made us?

I usually gag a bit when I hear someone offer words of encouragement like this, especially when I'm in the midst of some serious challenge or hurt. When I'm in pain, I don't want to hear, "It's all part of God's plan," "Don't worry, God will take care of you," or "Turn that frown upside down—Jesus loves you!"[43] These statements may be true; but more often than not, they come from someone who goes to the emergency room for a moderate hangnail. On the other hand, coming from James, these words have a whole different authority. He's writing this from the midst of his discomfort, while he and his people suffered. What sounds cheesy coming from the mouth of most people packs a powerful punch coming from James.

[43] Okay, I *never* ever want to hear that last one.

Another reason I can hear these words from James is that he doesn't just tell us to find joy in pain; he lets us know how pain can have positive results. Trials, tests of our faith, and even times of discipline[44] each play an important role in forming us into mature, complete people. So these words carry huge amounts of authority because they're coming from someone who has also "been there, done that" and knows what's on the other side. While we can become overly focused on our current difficulties and pain, James' words lift our heads up so we can see past the present unpleasantness and into the potential growth of the future.

[44] See Hebrews 12:5-12.

Soap Box

Sometimes I get the feeling that we expect God to take away all pain, discomfort, and inconvenience when we become Christians. It's like once we join the club, we should get a "fast pass" for the toll roads, butt to the front of the security lines at the airport, and even win free HBO. I'm not sure where these expectations come from, but I'm pretty sure it's not from the Bible. Through stories in both the Old and New Testaments and through the teachings of Jesus, Paul and James pick up just the opposite trend:

- You cannot get to the Promised Land except through the wilderness.
- You must sacrifice your only son before you can become the father of many nations.
- In order to save your family from famine, you need to be sold into slavery, be falsely accused of hitting on your boss' wife, and be thrown in prison.[45]

We need to listen to the wise words of the Dread Pirate Roberts: "Life is pain, Highness. Anyone who tells you different is selling something."[46] Jesus says something similar: "In this world you will have trouble. But take heart! I have overcome the world."[47]

We need to expect discomfort and disequilibrium[48] in our lives. As teachers and leaders, these challenges become valuable opportunities to encourage growth. If learning only happens through discomfort, then part of our job is to take advantage of and even create these moments.

Hebrews 10:24 discusses spurring one another on to love and good deeds. When I think of a spur, I imagine the metal attachments cowboys hook on their boot heels to encourage their horses to move. Spurs are hard and sometimes pointed. The whole idea of a spur is to make the horse uncomfortable, thus motivating it to ride. There's no such thing as "Nerf spurs."[49] They just couldn't do the job. So we have to make people uncomfortable if we're to "spur one another on."

[45] I'll let you figure out which biblical stories I'm referencing here. E-mail your answers to me (at BearLosey@sbcglobal.net), and I'll give you a totally worthless prize.

[46] From *The Princess Bride* (Twentieth Century Fox, 1987). The "Dread Pirate Roberts" should do a seminar on leadership principles.

[47] John 16:33.

[48] This may be a new idea for some, so there's more on disequilibrium in the next section.

[49] If there are Nerf spurs, they're not very effective. Thanks to Jack Hawkins for sharing the concept of Nerf spurs.

Disequilibrium

Disequilibrium can be an intimidating word. It's long, it sounds kind of Latin, and it even has a ***q*** in it.[50] But don't let these things scare you off. Understanding how disequilibrium works can revolutionize how you think about teaching and leading. Remember spinning around and around when you were a kid,[51] and then you'd stop and try to remain on your feet? The world kept spinning even after you'd stopped, and you'd stumble as you awkwardly tried to keep your feet under you. That's often what it feels like to experience a physical loss of equilibrium. Eventually the world stops spinning, and you're able to stand and walk straight again. We experience similar sensations emotionally, intellectually, and socially when our world is spun around.

Disequilibrium occurs when we encounter new and different forces or dynamics. In order to reestablish equilibrium, we must either create ways to deal with the strange, new situation, or we must deny its existence. Denial usually leads us toward ways to isolate and create a protective shell around the new situation so we can continue to use our old skills and perspectives and don't have to integrate the new situation into our lives.

There are times when denial is essential to our survival, such as when it serves to protect us. Extreme situations for which we're poorly equipped and when there's little time to gain new skills require us to ignore the new situation just to survive.[52]

[50] For some reason a word containing the letter q is a bit more impressive—"qualitative analysis," "ubiquitous," etc.

[51] Or last week.

[52] This often happens in abuse situations and trauma. In order to survive, we protect ourselves from the things we don't have the ability to handle yet. We create a "lacuna," or gap in our thinking, and surround it with protective behaviors and thoughts so we don't have to address the gap.

Denial becomes debilitating when it's not addressed. When life gets more normal, we can and should go back and deal with the denial. This can be difficult to do when we don't know that we've denied a situation and may require professional help.[53] More often we acknowledge the new situation and begin to explore ways to deal with it. We begin to stumble around, practicing new skills that will help us integrate the new forces and dynamics into our lives. Gradually these new skills become a part of us and how we live.

[53] It's important that you understand the limits of your training and experience as a teacher or leader. If you're not a trained counselor or therapist, keep a referral list. Don't "unpack" what you can't "repack."

Disequilibrium distinguishes being uncomfortable from a discomfort that leads to growth. A rock in your shoe is uncomfortable, but it doesn't necessarily throw you into disequilibrium. Running into an old boyfriend may be awkward, but this unexpected meeting probably doesn't require new coping skills. But starting at a new school or even getting a new dog will demand new skills and insights. Discomfort, trials, or challenges that spin your world around—in big or little ways—create the disequilibrium that can lead to growth and development. Being able to tell the difference between discomfort and disequilibrium helps you notice and take advantage of these amazing learning opportunities.

The Importance of Being Out of Your Depth

> **When** you pass through the waters, I will be with you; and **when** you pass through the rivers, they will not sweep over you. **When** you walk through the fire, you will not be burned; the flames will not set you ablaze (Isaiah 43:2, **emphasis mine**).

Notice in this verse the expectation of walking through rivers and fire. It's not ***if*** you'll encounter obstacles—it's **when**. There's no question that things are going to get rough.[54] According to James and the author of Hebrews, trials are essential for learning and growth, building endurance, and spurring one another on. Yet it seems most of us do all we can to avoid or ignore the situations that Scripture says we should not only expect, but also consider as the very things we need for growth.

[54] Yet it seems we live with the exact opposite assumption: *Things should never get tough for a believer.* We seem shocked and surprised when we encounter difficult situations—even when they're of our own making.

I taught swimming lessons for several years. Working with the preschool kids was challenging but always entertaining. Some were terrified of the water,[55] but there were always at least a few kids who couldn't wait to get in and learn to swim. These "water lovers" must have had older siblings or parents who liked the water because they'd sit on the pool steps—in water that barely covered their knees—and do their best imitations of real swimming with arms swinging wildly and exaggerated head turns and breathing. They looked like Olympic athletes in training. (Of course their feet were still planted on the bottom of the pool, and more than half of their bodies were still above the surface.) I cheered them on, gave pointers, and tried to improve their techniques.

[55] While some of the kids had a real fear of the water, most of the wailing and crying was due to missing their parents or having wet pants that were not of their own doing.

While these arm and head movements are all important parts of learning how to swim, it's not actually swimming. Not yet anyway. I'd be a terrible swim instructor if I stopped there. At some point I needed to take these kids into a part of the pool where they couldn't touch the bottom. It's only when they're in the deep water that they can see how their kicking and arm motions will keep them on top of the water and moving forward. If they never took their feet off the bottom of the pool, they'd never learn to swim. In life we also need to get out of our depth and over our heads—and on a regular basis—if we're going to learn how to stay afloat.

And if we really want to help teenagers grow and mature in their faith, then we need to learn how to guide them safely through the deep waters in their lives. Just like a lifeguard or a wilderness guide, this type of training requires a skill set that needs intentional development and maintenance. Understanding and using the concept of "comfort zones" is one of the most important skills we need if we're to help students learn and grow through disequilibrium.

Comfort Zones

I hear the term ***comfort zone*** a ton. When I'm leading workshops or training teams, we talk about goals and ground rules. So at almost every event, I hear people talk about being "out of their comfort zones" or "discovering their comfort zones." When I ask what ***comfort zone*** means, the response I receive most often is a blank stare. Once the uncomfortable silence is finally overcome, the first replay is usually the obvious: "Isn't that the place where you're comfortable?"[56] That lets me know how specific they are in their requests. While they know of the need to be made uncomfortable in order to grow, they aren't aware that there's a more specific meaning and application of comfort zones.

[56] This response is usually offered by someone who has a keen grasp of the obvious.

If you need to be outside your comfort zone to grow, then you need to know when you cross that line and enter into disequilibrium—a new zone where learning and growth happen. A deeper understanding of comfort zones can help you safely lead people through disequilibrium to learning and growth.

Figure 4
Comfort Zone

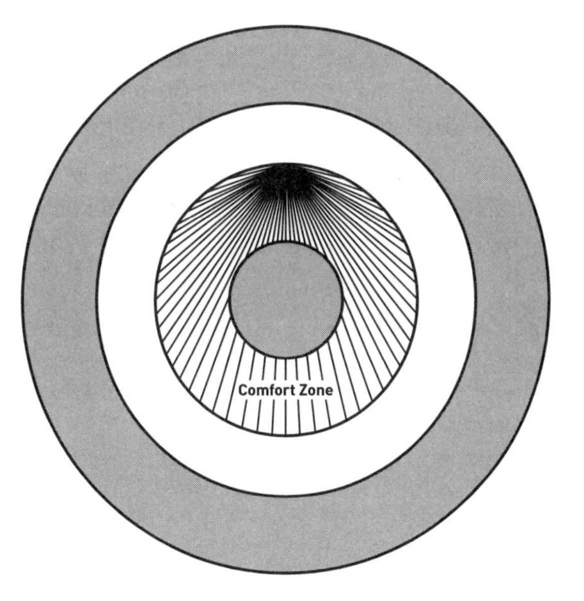

The Comfort Zone

Comfort zones are often pictured as a dartboard divided into a number of different fields (figure 4). Each field (or zone) represents a different comfort level accompanied by behaviors, emotions, and challenges.

Let's start with the zone for which this model is named—The Comfort Zone. As we've already established, the most obvious but least helpful definition is "the zone where we feel most comfortable." Other possible definitions are "doing things we've done before" or "being in a place that's familiar." In other words, we definitely feel comfortable in these situations. However, that doesn't mean we're automatically in disequilibrium whenever we don't feel comfortable, or we find ourselves in a new situation.

As a traveling trainer, I'm often in places and situations I've never encountered before. But these new environments don't always require new skills or perspectives, either. So while entering these unfamiliar areas isn't always easy for me, I'm not necessarily thrown into disequilibrium. Thus, if exiting your comfort zone implies entering disequilibrium, then new locations or situations don't define the boundary lines.

Comfort zones have less to do with where we are or what we're doing than ***how we see our likelihood of success or failure***. As long as I believe my chances for success are better than my chances for failure, then I'm still inside my comfort zone. But as soon as the possibility of failure turns into the ***probability*** of failure, I've left my comfort zone.[57]

I teach scuba diving off the coast of Southern California. While the beaches can be warm and inviting, scuba diving from them can be a bit...exciting. The same waves that make surfers salivate, scuba divers dread.[58] The water is cold and even past the waves it can surge several feet at a time. If you can shore dive off the coast of Southern California, you can scuba dive almost anywhere.

While diving in Costa Rica, we planned a boat trip to the Catalina Islands.[59] The dive master warned us of the difficult diving conditions and extreme currents. We took his warning seriously, but we were also confident of our skills. Even though I was in a new location and diving situation, I was still very comfortable with the dive. I knew my chances of having a successful dive were good, and I didn't feel I was lacking any skills or perspectives. I was ***not*** outside my comfort zone.

I exited my comfort zone during a different diving situation, however. I spent a few years working for a company that did marine science research and education off the coasts of California and Hawaii. I worked off a large boat and did hundreds of dives off the Channel Islands in California. One time my dive buddy and I were returning from a collection dive[60] when the captain asked us to check the anchor. He said it was at about 60 or 70 feet and he just wanted us to make sure it was secure on the bottom. I was low on air, but I thought I had enough for a quick trip down and then a slow trip up. The anchor turned out to be below 80 feet. This took more air than I had anticipated. After I checked the anchor, I tried to take a breath from my regulator and there was nothing there. I was more than 80 feet deep, my dive buddy was 10 yards away, and I had no air. While I didn't exactly panic, I assessed my chances for survival at less than 50 percent.

I'd been diving in this location many times; and while I'd been trained in emergency ascents, I'd never actually done a real one. I was outside my comfort zone, and I had to acquire and apply new skills immediately. I executed an emergency swimming ascent and made it to the surface with no ill effects, other than an amazing

[57] In my view, as soon as a person's perspective of the possibility of failure passes 50 percent, he's probably experiencing disequilibrium.

[58] Entering the water from the beach can be painful and expensive as big waves pummel you and then your gear scatters and gets washed out to sea.

[59] Not Catalina Island off the coast of Southern California, by the way. Costa Rica has its own Catalina Islands.

[60] Part of my job was to catch marine life to use while teaching on the boat. I had all the proper collection permits and returned the creatures back to the water after we finished with them.

adrenaline rush and a new appreciation for my scuba instructors. Even though I was in a familiar place, I found myself in a situation where I thought my chances of success were slim. I was in disequilibrium.

In order for the concept of a comfort zone to be helpful, it must tell us more about when we enter a state of disequilibrium than when we're uncomfortable. The comfort zone is defined as where we see our chances of success as probable. Failure is still a possibility but not likely. Here we feel confident, safe, and willing to take risks. It's where we live most of the time and ***incorporate*** what we've learned, but it's not ***where*** we learn.

Figure 5
Growth Zone

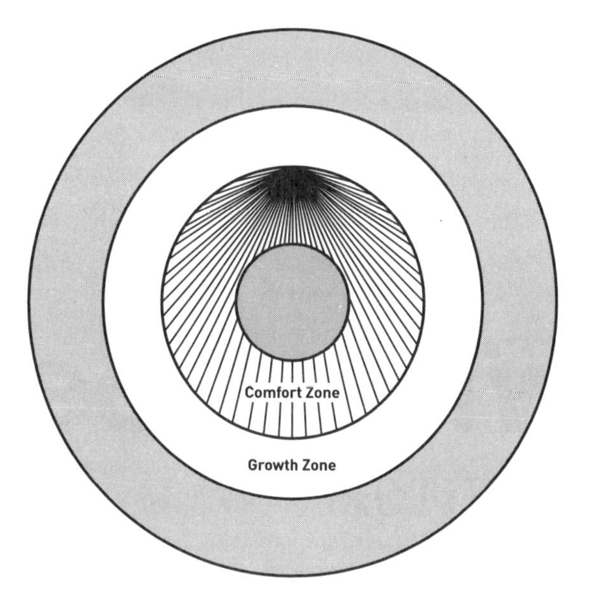

The Growth Zone

As soon as we find ourselves outside our comfort zones and in disequilibrium, we must either develop or deny.[61] This is where learning and growth happen (figure 5). As we confront our limitations and the probability of failure, we're challenged to discover new ways to live and to see the world. Stepping into this zone is scary; staying in the growth zone for any length of time is exhausting. Why would people do this to themselves on purpose?

[61] Turn back a few pages and review the "Disequilibrium" section in this chapter.

Leaving our comfort zones for the unknown territory of the growth zone is difficult. Few of us can take this step on our own. We may be willing and excited to learn, but it's difficult for us to see our own limitations until we've gone beyond them. Often we only discover we need to grow when we notice we're uncomfortable, look failure in the face, and admit it to ourselves. Then we look back to see just when we left our comfort zones and how exposed we really are. We don't step boldly into the growth zone, but we find ourselves already there—if not by accident, then at least not of our own accord.

Even though we tend not to enter the growth zone voluntarily, we can be purposeful and intentional when we do find ourselves there. The first thing to do is to ***recognize and admit where you are.***

I was leading a group of college student leaders on a six-day backpacking trip. The first five days were fun, challenging, and a great learning experience; but the last night proved to be the most powerful. We'd cached our last meal along the trail so we wouldn't have to carry it the whole way.[62] When we stopped to set up camp, I sent three volunteers back up the trail to pick up our food. This should have taken less than an hour; yet two hours later, only two of the three students walked back into camp. I asked them where the third student, Bill, was. The other two explained that after an hour of walking without finding the cache, they'd said they should head back. However, Bill, a former Boy Scout,[63] was convinced he knew where the food was, so he wanted to keep going. Thus, the two turned back for camp, and Bill kept searching.

I was furious with the other two for letting Bill continue hiking alone. A big part of my anger stemmed from my fear of having one of my students lost in the backcountry. But Bill's biggest problem wasn't ***being*** lost; it was ***not knowing*** he was lost. He kept walking up the trail until the sun started to go down behind the mountains. As the light dimmed, it finally dawned on him that he was lost. At that point he did the correct thing: He sat down and waited until morning.[64]

Bill couldn't do anything until he acknowledged he was lost. Once he did so, he began to take the necessary steps for being found. Once we find ourselves in the growth zone, we must acknowledge where we are before we can begin to learn. If we never stop and humbly admit we're in over our heads, we can never take advantage of the great lessons available to us.

[62] "Caching food" means to hang it in a tree out of the reach (hopefully) of bears and other critters. This way we didn't have to carry the weight of the food, and we could still have a wonderful gourmet pasta meal out on the trail.

[63] Who should have known better than to hike alone.

[64] That evening I ran up and down the trail from the camp to the cache several times without finding him, and I spent a sleepless night worrying about him. The next morning I found a few people on horseback to help us search, but Bill walked into camp an hour after first light.

Three Growth Inhibitors

Several factors keep us from admitting we need to grow:[65] Fear of failure,[66] pride, or just plain ignorance. Whichever one keeps us from acknowledging we're in the growth zone cannot be ignored, but it must be owned and embraced. It's only in claiming our fear or our pride that we can move past it. Knowing our limitations doesn't commit us to them, but it teaches us how to overcome them.[67]

Owning the fear and anxiety that comes with finding ourselves in the growth zone helps us take advantage of our visit there. Even while we're firmly established in our comfort zones, we may still know that we need to grow. But in the growth zone, we become aware of our limits and what our next steps in growth can be. We begin to realize failure is essential to learning, and it can be valued. The growth zone reveals to us exactly where we're lacking and offers direction and purpose in our efforts to learn.

[65] This is not an exhaustive list.

[66] Or just fear.

[67] We could never have put a man on the moon without knowing about gravity.

Maximizing the Growth Zone

As we help teenagers step out of their comfort zones and into the growth zone, our primary tasks should be creating environments where our kids are valued—even when they fail—and encouraged to try new things. Henri Nouwen defines the givers of such help as ones who "offer a free and friendly place where one has to discover his own lonely way."[68] The best way we can help people find themselves in the growth zone is to create safe places where they can try things they believe are unsafe, and they can risk failure without risking loss of acceptance[69]—places where they're reminded that their value isn't based on success or their accomplishments, but on the heavenly price that has already been paid.[70] Our job as youth workers is to create this kind of place and to model learning and failing.

[68] From the foreword to *Reaching Out: The Three Movements of the Spiritual Life* (New York: Doubleday, 1975).

[69] Notice I didn't say, "risk failure without the consequences." The consequences of our failures are what teach us the lessons. Failure without consequences isn't reality—it's video games.

[70] 1 Corinthians 7:23—That price being the Christ. Your value has been set. You're worth the price of the Son of God!

Soap Box

It's only in the growth zone that our faith becomes real and useful. John Ortberg once told my adventure program staff that we only know our faith by using it. For instance, our faith in God is pleasant and reassuring when we're in our comfort zone; it becomes essential when we enter the growth zone. We can no longer rely on our own skills and insights, and we must trust that God is in control and will provide what we need: "Now to him who is able to do immeasurably more than all we ask or imagine, according to his power that is at work within us" (Ephesians 3:20). If you really want to know your faith, you need to stop avoiding what you fear and trust that God isn't threatened by what threatens you.

Comfort zone theory also offers insight into where we don't grow.

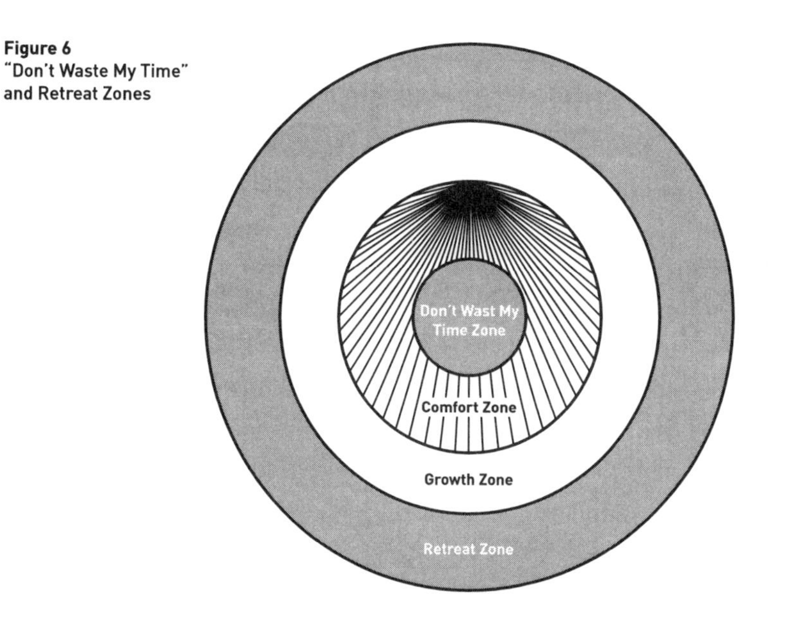

Figure 6
"Don't Waste My Time" and Retreat Zones

The Retreat Zone and the "Don't Waste My Time" Zone

When we're in one of these next two zones, not only do we not grow, but we also become frustrated and may even take a few steps backward.

Just outside the growth zone is a place where we cannot imagine ourselves being successful (figure 6)—**The Retreat Zone**. In the growth zone, we still have hope that we may succeed and gain new skills and insights. But once we let go of that last thread of hope, we enter the retreat zone, where we're more likely to see zero percent chance of success. We typically find ourselves in this zone after being confronted with an impossible situation or by staying in the growth zone too long, where fatigue eventually drains all hope from us and changes a potential learning situation into a depressing and destructive experience. First we tend to deny or despair, then, as the name implies, we retreat to a place where our current skill set works.

Once someone enters the retreat zone, he either shuts down entirely or becomes angry, aggressive, or frustrated. Either he curls up in the fetal position, or he lashes out like a cornered wildcat. Any of these responses has the same result: The retreat-er "buys out" and is no longer engaged. When we find one of our students (or ourselves) in this situation, she must return to the comfort zone as soon as possible. There may be wounds that need to heal and trust may need to be restored. Hope is restored and healing can happen when people see themselves as successful and comfortable.

Deep inside our comfort zones there is a place where we become bored—so bored, in fact, that we're not only disengaged, but also offended by the situation. Now we're in the **"Don't Waste My Time" Zone**. This occurs when we're supposed to be learning, but we're offered a "challenge" that's so simple it's demeaning.

For example, imagine you're at a daylong math workshop.[71] The leader begins by holding up both hands, each with the pointer finger raised.

[71] I'm sure just the thought of this pushed some of you into your retreat zone.

"Okay, class. How many fingers am I holding up on my right hand? One. Good job! Now how many fingers am I holding up on my left hand? One. Excellent! Now if I take the number of fingers on my right hand and ***add*** it to the number of fingers on my left hand, how many fingers am I holding up? Two. So how many fingers do I have up on both hands altogether? Two. Way to go!"

Imagine this goes on for an entire hour. You glance at the day's agenda and see that the whole morning will be dedicated to simple addition; and, if that's mastered, the afternoon will be dedicated to subtraction. You may find yourself in your growth zone if you happen to be in elementary school, but my guess is that this subject matter is already well within your comfort zone.

Now imagine this workshop is being offered at an engineering conference. Words like ***insulting***, ***demeaning***, and ***a waste of time*** describe the thoughts of the poor professionals trapped in that seminar. When our time is being wasted, we either clam up or lash out. We become frustrated, offended, and angry.

Notice that the outward signs of the "don't waste my time" zone and the retreat zone are the same: We'll know which zone we find ourselves in, but we won't always know what zone others are occupying.

I was once leading a women's athletic team through the Spider Web, a classic initiative activity,[72] when I noticed one of the women was standing off to the side. She was leaning against a tree with her arms folded across her chest. She had a blank, disinterested look on her face, and she didn't speak at all as the group worked on the problem. I knew that, physically speaking, this activity was well within her abilities, so I assumed the problem-solving aspect of the challenge wasn't engaging her. So in an attempt to pull her back in, I increased the challenge by not letting them use some of the larger openings in the web. This would force the group to lift each other up to get through the web, thereby increasing their need to rely on each other. It would also force them to touch each other more.

[72] See the Activity section in my book *The Experiential Youth Ministry Handbook*. Yes, this is a shameless plug.

The woman standing by the tree took off. The new rules I'd added turned out to be too much for her, so she just left. My assumption that this was a "don't waste my time" zone issue was way off. ***If I'd simply asked her, then I would've found out she had a huge problem with people touching her. The truth was she'd been driven deep into her retreat zone by the additional challenge.***

It's important to realize that—outwardly—the retreat zone and the "don't waste my time" zone look very similar, yet they're exact opposite situations that require very different responses. So the fact that they look so similar creates a huge challenge for leaders and teachers. We can't assume we know where people are at just by observing their postures, attitudes, or words.

Fortunately, the confusion between these zones can easily be cleared up by simply asking people how they're doing and by double-checking our assumptions before acting. We must face the challenge of learning the subtle clues that differentiate them and having the courage to ask the simple question: "How are you doing?"

Figure 7
Overview of the Zones

Comfort Zone Theory Overview

- **Don't Waste My Time Zone:** Participants aren't challenged at all. They're not even close to the limits of their abilities. "Buy Out," frustration, and boredom are the marks of the "Don't Waste My Time" Zone.

- **Comfort Zone:** Participants feel safe and within the limits of their abilities. They may even feel challenged, but still within what they think is possible. Stability and security are the marks of the Comfort Zone.

- **Growth Zone:** Participants feel unsettled and outside the limits of their abilities. They're just outside the Comfort Zone. The challenge they feel is beyond what they expected. Anxiety, fear, and instability are the marks of the Growth Zone.

- **Retreat Zone:** Participants feel extreme fear and anxiety—to the point of hopelessness. They're so far beyond what they feel they're capable of doing, they abandon the desire to even try. "Buy Out," frustration, failure, and boredom are the marks of the Retreat Zone.

Participants are always in a dynamic state. They move in and out of these zones as conditions and situations change.

Implications and Applications

Now that we've laid out the different areas found in Comfort Zone Theory (figure 7), there are a few more details that can make this information even more useful. Like a map, comfort zones can be used as a decoration—a pretty picture that hangs on the wall and adds to the aesthetics of the room. Also like a map, if you take the time to learn how to use the different zones, it can help you "find yourself," understand where you've been, and chart a course for where you wish to go. A skilled leader can identify when people move into the growth zone, guide them away from retreat, and challenge them to step out of the comfort zone. By knowing where our students are, we can point them in a beneficial direction so their next steps are toward growth.

This is where using Comfort Zone Theory becomes art. You've been given the brushes, the pigment, and a few brushstrokes to use; now you need to use them if you're going to understand how to paint. By looking at individuals or groups through the lens of Comfort Zone Theory, you'll be able to take advantage of the insights it offers. Learning may happen in the growth zone, but the lessons can't be integrated into a person's life until he gets back to his comfort zone, where he'll have a chance to recover from the experience and reflect on the lesson.

Some people lift weights to get in shape. The workout challenges the muscles to new levels of work, and this challenge requires new growth. But the growth happens as the muscles rest. That's why you don't work out the same muscles every day. If you did, the muscles would never recover, and you'd never get in shape.

The same is true for life in the growth zone. The challenges we face that move us into the growth zone require the same opportunity to recover as our muscles do. We cannot live in the growth zone for too long before the lessons we encounter there overwhelm us and push us into retreat. The skilled leader not only leads people into the growth zone but also has the wisdom to know when to lead them back to the comfort zone.

The learning process becomes a dance where the student steps into the growth zone, gains new skills and insights, and is led back to his comfort zone where those skills are integrated into his life. When he's rested and recovered, he's then challenged to step back out for more growth. The art is to know when a person or group starts to fatigue in the growth zone, when to lead them back, and what form the next challenge should take. Just as the painter only discovers her painting style ***by painting***, you'll discover how Comfort Zone Theory works by trying it out in your unique context, playing with it, and paying attention to the results (figure 8).

Figure 8
Where learning happens

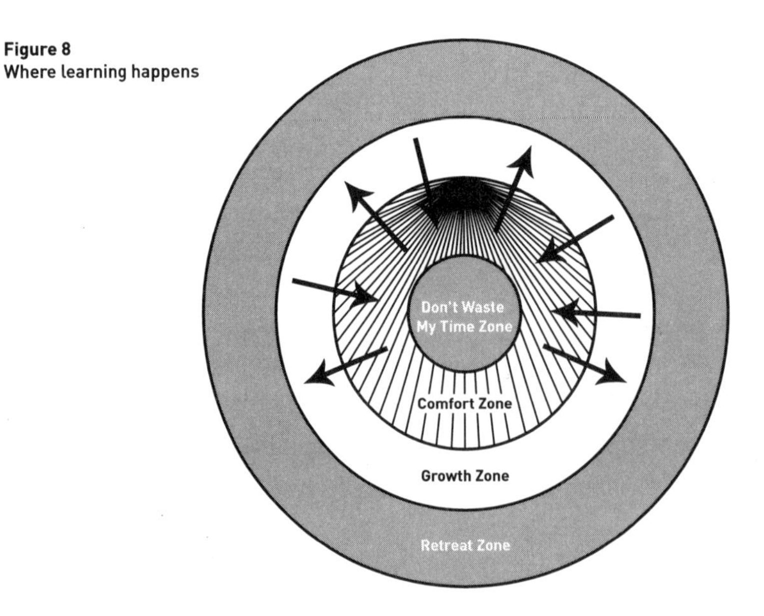

SPHERES OF GROWTH

Chapter 1.3

I studied biology in college.[73] As I started my classes, one of the things that excited me most was the prospect of doing dissections—cutting things open and poking around inside. However, I soon discovered that dissection is more difficult than I'd thought. We'd cut up frogs and cats in high school, and that's where we started in my first college zoology class;[74] the difference was in the required detail and the fact that we were supposed to use the dissection to study. I couldn't just hack up an animal, pin things back, and turn it in. We'd spend several weeks on each dissection, slowly revealing and exploring different systems and tissues. I did okay with the larger specimens: frogs, cats, and even a shark. But things changed when we started working with invertebrates: worms, snails, and other creepy crawlies.

[73] Not just a class or two. I have a bachelor's degree in biology.

[74] More on that first frog later.

Then I was given a large earthworm to study.[75] As an example, the professor showed us a completed dissection; it was beautiful. Really. The skin was artfully laid back to reveal rings of muscle, and several different tubes and vessels were each separated and labeled. It should have been displayed in the lobby as art.

[75] *Large* being a relative term. For a worm, it was huge; but let's be real—it was still a worm.

I was excited to start this project. I organized my dissection kit, carefully laid the worm in a dissection pan, picked up my scalpel, and made my first cut. Goo. All I revealed was gelatinous ooze that could only be labeled "goo." I tried to carefully poke around to reveal the different organs; but the more I poked, the more "goo-like" the worm became.[76] My specimen was now worthless for study because I couldn't identify any distinct parts; I couldn't see any differences, so I didn't gain any additional understanding.

[76] My next project was a garden snail. The results were more "snot-like" than "goo-like."

Dissection is essential in order to understand organisms. We tend to take the same approach to understanding almost everything—we like to break it down into pieces. We learn to read by breaking a word down into syllables and sounding them out. If you want to learn how to repair a machine, you start by taking one apart. We learn concepts, cars, and caterpillars all by dissection. We can also gain a greater insight into people by understanding them as a complex collection of different parts. This is the essence of Wellness Theory.

What Is "Wellness"?

It looks at people as a collection of different components that all need attention. Health care and recreation professionals use this idea to encourage people to be more active and improve their diets so they don't neglect the physical aspect of their beings. Increasingly we're hearing human resources people talk about "corporate wellness," the idea that people will work better if they do more than just sit behind a desk. The same is being done at universities. Students are encouraged not only to excel in their studies, but also to take care of themselves physically, emotionally, spiritually, and socially.[77] The "wellness wheel" is popping up both in health care brochures and on student life Web sites. The idea is that if we understand the different components that make us healthy people, we'll be better able to care for ourselves, to create programs that increase the quality of our lives, and ultimately to be better people. Nontraditional medicines and other holistic approaches have also claimed Wellness Theory as their own. But this is not a new concept. The Bible addressed this idea 2,000 years ago.

[77] I use these five areas: intellectual, physical, social, emotional, and spiritual/moral. The specifics of wellness will be discussed later in this section.

The Bible and Wellness

Throughout Scripture, many ideas and word pictures rely on the concept of wellness—the idea that one thing consists of several important parts, essentially different but equal in value. "One body with many parts" is a phrase repeatedly used by Paul in his letters.[78] Jesus talks about the vine and the branches.[79] Even the concept of the Trinity relies on wellness for understanding.

[78] Romans 12; 1 Corinthians 10 and 12; Ephesians 2; Colossians 3.

[79] John 15.

When Jesus is asked to discuss the greatest commandment, he uses the concept of wellness to express the importance of dedicating our whole selves to God: "Love the Lord your God with all your **heart** and with all your **soul** and with all your **mind** and with all your **strength**" (Mark 12:30, **emphasis added**).[80]

[80] Also see Luke 10:27.

Paul emphasizes the importance of addressing the whole person in his closing remarks to the Thessalonians: "May God himself, the God of peace, sanctify you through and through. May your whole **spirit, soul, and body** be kept blameless at the coming of our Lord Jesus Christ" (1 Thessalonians 5:23, **emphasis added**).

Paul also stresses the importance of and unique role each part plays:

> Now the body is not made up of one part but of many. If the foot should say, "Because I am not a hand, I do not belong to the body," it would not for that reason cease to be part of the body. And if the ear should say, "Because I am not an eye, I do not belong to the body," it would not for that reason cease to be part of the body. If the whole body were an eye, where would the sense of hearing be? If the whole body were an ear, where would the sense of smell be? But in fact God has arranged the parts in the body, every one of them, just as he wanted them to be. If they were all one part, where would the body be? As it is, there are many parts, but one body. The eye cannot say to the hand, "I don't need you!" And the head cannot say to the feet, "I don't need you!" On the contrary, those parts of the body that seem to be weaker are indispensable, and the parts that we

> think are less honorable we treat with special honor. And the parts that are unpresentable are treated with special modesty, while our presentable parts need no special treatment. But God has combined the members of the body and has given greater honor to the parts that lacked it, so that there should be no division in the body, but that its parts should have equal concern for each other. If one part suffers, every part suffers with it; if one part is honored, every part rejoices with it.—1 Corinthians 12:14-26

The difference between the parts is not only true, it's also an asset. There is strength and flexibility in the diversity of parts. Paul also acknowledges the different ways we view parts—some have special honor or modesty. But the way each part is treated doesn't change its importance or how it impacts all the other parts.

It's important for us as teachers and leaders to understand the importance of each aspect of a teenager. No matter how you label the parts—"heart, soul, mind, strength," "spirit, soul and body," or other titles—each part is essential.

Soap Box

Too often in ministry we see ourselves as being responsible for impacting only the spiritual lives of our people. We place a premium on spiritual development, usually at the exclusion of offering leadership in other areas. Either we believe that other aspects of life aren't as valuable as spirituality, or we don't believe we have permission to encourage people to grow in areas other than spiritual ones. Paul debunks both of those myths.

The 1 Corinthians passage stresses the importance of all aspects of a body, whether it's a church or a person. Then in the book of Colossians, Paul talks about his goals in ministry: "We proclaim him, admonishing and teaching everyone with all wisdom, so that we may present everyone perfect in Christ. To this end I labor, struggling with all his energy, which so powerfully works in me" (Colossians 1:28-29). When Paul talks about presenting people "perfect," he uses the word ***teleios***, which refers to completeness, wholeness, or maturity.[81] His work involves all aspects of a person. Paul doesn't limit his efforts to the spiritual life. He seeks to present complete people—people who are fully mature in all areas of their lives. If we view our ministerial roles in this context, then gaining an understanding of Wellness Theory becomes vitally important.

[81] *Strong's Talking Greek & Hebrew Dictionary* by James Strong (Ontario, Canada: Online Bible, 1993).

The Wellness Concept

People can be understood as consisting of a complex combination of different areas or needs. The Wellness Concept encourages us to tend to all these areas and seek balance and harmony in our lives. This may sound a bit "crunchy,"[82] but it does make sense. If you eat Jack-in-the-Box three meals a day, every day, you won't feel well. If you play video games five hours a day and never go outside or pick up a book, your life will not be very rich.[83]

[82] *Crunchy* refers to granola, earthy, or "New Age," but it's not as scary for many evangelical Christians.

[83] Reading outside is one of my favorite things to do.

There isn't anything mystical or spooky about wellness. It just points out that we're made up of different parts, and we need to pay attention to all of them. For the Wellness Concept to be useful, we need to choose how we'll "dissect" ourselves and decide what to call the parts we create. The Bible uses "spirit, soul and body"[84] and also "heart, soul, mind, and strength."[85] Some contemporary models of wellness include areas such as occupational, financial, environmental, and nutritional.[86]

[84] 1 Thessalonians 5:23.

[85] Mark 12:30.

[86] I checked out some Web sites on wellness and found some that have more than 30 different areas.

Figure 9
The Wellness Wheel

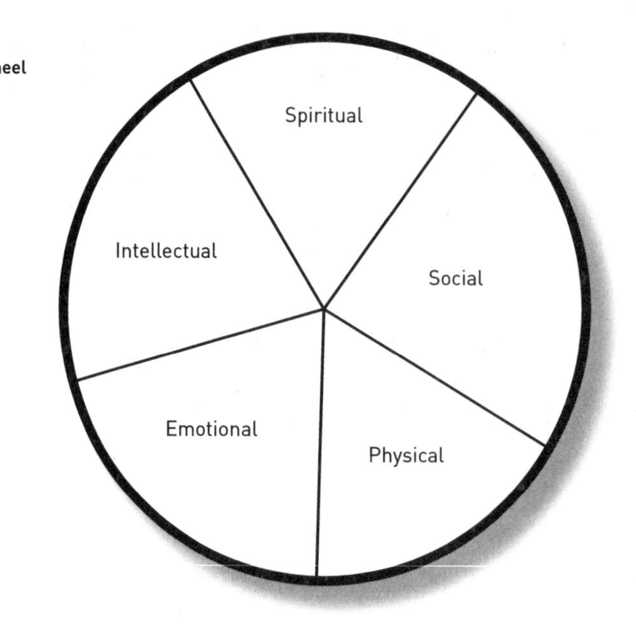

The Wellness Wheel

Regardless of how many areas a model uses, this "Wellness Wheel" is by far the most common model used to understand this concept (figure 9). The areas are arranged in a circle with each one forming a spoke of a wheel. For a wheel to function, all the spokes must be adjusted to keep the wheel balanced. The picture of a functioning wheel is useful no matter how many spokes you use in your wellness model. The three areas of body, mind, and spirit create a simple wheel with three spokes. It's easy to understand, but it creates such large parts that it's difficult to put into action. A wheel with 30 spokes is specific and detailed, but it may create a complexity that is confusing and just as difficult to put into practice. Of the many useful models I've seen, I choose to use a wheel of five spokes: Intellectual, Physical, Social, Emotional, and Spiritual (or moral).

Intellectual

Tending to intellectual wellness includes activities that stimulate thought and learning. School and study are the classic ways this area is addressed. We need to continue to challenge ourselves to new perspectives and to deeper understanding. It's important that we continue to gather information and learn ways to apply that information to creatively solve problems.

Physical

Physical wellness involves our body—its movement, what we put into it, and how it develops. Our minds may make a plan, but our bodies carry out that plan. Physical activity and nutrition are major concerns in this area. Recreation and physical play have very important roles. Fine motor skills and the physical aspects of problem solving are also vital to continued wellness in this area.

Social

The social aspect of wellness involves the interactions we share with the people around us—we exist in the context of community. Sometimes this area of wellness is referred to as "interpersonal" because of its emphasis on the interdependent nature of communities. Communication, listening, and understanding the implications of your actions on the people around you are all part of developing this area.

Emotional

Emotions and feelings play an important part in our overall wellness, yet the importance of this area is often ignored or diminished. How we feel impacts how we see the world and what we think of it. Our emotions and moods can impact how we deal with stress and how we function in difficult situations.

Spiritual (Moral)

Exploring the meaning and purpose of life is the realm of spiritual and moral wellness. Everyone has a spiritual component. You don't need to be involved in a church or another organized religion to wrestle with the core questions of life's meaning and purpose—what's right and wrong. Confronting and addressing ethical dilemmas and exploring core beliefs and assumptions offer opportunities to develop spiritual wellness.

Pie Versus Prism

While the Wellness Wheel is the most common picture used to understand wellness, a pie can also be a useful similar image. A person starts off being seen as a whole—like a fresh pie right out of the oven. To gain access to the pie, we cut it into pieces and serve those pieces. How many pieces we cut is up to the person doing the cutting. They'll cut the pie into sections that best fit their needs. Whether it's cut into three pieces or 30 pieces isn't as important as getting access to the pie. Each slice of the pie can now be served individually.

The pie picture is helpful in several ways. It reminds us that we cut the pie into pieces that suit our needs. It gives us a picture of acknowledging and addressing the different areas of an individual. It also reminds us of some of the dangers of the Wellness Concept. For instance, sometimes we forget that the pie pieces started out as a whole. We also might get so caught up in the distribution of the individual pieces that we forget that we did the cutting.

Remember me dissecting frogs? Let's go back to that zoology lab. The first quarter or semester for almost any college major contains at least one "weeder" class—a class designed to discourage any students who aren't serious about their studies. The biology program at Cal Poly, San Luis Obispo, had such a class—Zoo 131 taught by Dr. De Jong. The first day of this course was intimidating. As soon as we settled into our seats, our eyes gleamed with anticipation—as only incoming freshmen's eyes can look. Then Dr. De Jong passed out a thick 40-page handout[87] packed with charts, graphs, equations, and other scientific information.

[87] And it was single-spaced and printed on both sides.

He held up a copy and said, "This handout contains the information I assume you already know. This is the only time I'll refer to it in class, but you'll be expected to know and be responsible for all of it." He tossed it onto his desk, and then he started his first lecture. The gleam in our eyes soon changed to wide-eyed shock and distress.[88]

[88] This distress was magnified when he explained how we could get negative scores on his tests. (E-mail me at BearLosey@sbcglobal.net, and I'll tell you about it.)

Zoo 131 consisted of three lectures and a pair of three-hour labs each week. Our next meeting was our first lab session. Most of us had recovered from the shock and intensity of the first lecture, and I was looking forward to the lab. This is where we got to do dissections—we got to cut things up! As we walked into the room, I noticed lab tables with four chairs positioned around each one. I also noticed that each table held a terrarium containing two very large frogs.

We all sat down, and the lab professor performed all the preliminary duties that need to be done at the first meeting of any class: Who was and wasn't enrolled, necessary equipment, the major assignments, and how we'd be graded. This lasted for about 30 minutes. When she finished with the preliminaries, she asked us to put all the paperwork away, take out a pen and a blank piece of paper, and take a close look at the frogs in front of us.

Our assignment was to write down everything we noticed about these frogs. We could make a list or write in full sentences, but we had to be thorough. With the eagerness of new freshmen, we began writing. After about five minutes, I had a list of around 20 things, such as it's green, it has black and brown spots, it has two eyes, and so on. I looked around the lab and most people were still writing, but a few were looking around like me. Ten minutes later I had a few more things—four legs, a big funky-looking mouth.

The professor noticed several of us had our pens down and were looking around, so she encouraged us to keep going. Two hours later, after encouraging us several more times to keep writing, the professor reminded us to be sure to bring all our lab supplies and lab notebooks to the next class. Then she dismissed us. Several students commented on the strange lab assignment, but I assumed we'd received this assignment because few of us had our dissecting kits, and she wanted us to cut up the frogs together.

Two days later we walked back into the lab for the next session. We'd all brought our dissecting kits and lab notebooks. I was ready to tear into that frog.[89] I sat at the table with my new lab partner, set my dissecting kit on the table, and looked at the professor like a starving man at the dinner table. The professor asked us to take out

[89] In the name of science and education, of course.

the papers we'd been working on during the last lab session and to open up our new lab notebooks.

"Look at the list you made during the last lab. I want you to look closely at the frogs and write down everything you didn't notice the last time." I was caught off guard. We spent two hours making the first list. How could I have missed anything? But being a dutiful student[90] I took a closer look. To my surprise, I did notice some things I'd missed. The frog had only three toes on its front left foot. It had a clear membrane that covered each eye. Then again, after about five minutes, I lost steam.

[90] Hah!

I began to feel a bit frustrated that we weren't getting to do the dissection. And I could sense I was not alone in my frustration. You could feel the tension in the room rise as the time dragged on. After about 30 minutes, a student at another table spoke out.[91]

[91] I was too much of a wimp to express my frustration.

"Excuse me, professor. Isn't this supposed to be a biology lab? Aren't we supposed to dissect frogs? This assignment makes me feel like an English major or even an art major."[92]

[92] Two majors that incoming science students thought were beneath them.

Calmly, the professor responded, "Yes, this is a biology lab; and yes, we'll be dissecting these frogs in this class. In fact, you'll dissect many different specimens during your career as a biology student and a scientist. This assignment exercises one of the most important skills you'll need as a scientist: Observation. It also reminds us all of something that will serve you well as a biologist and as a person."

She picked up a prepared frog dissection in one hand and a living frog in the other and asked, "Which of these is a frog?"

A bit confused, a few students raised their hands and said, "Both are."

"No," she said. She held up the living frog and said, "This is the frog. It is whole. It is living, breathing, moving, eating. It is alive." Holding up the prepared dissection, she then said, "This is frog parts. Once you begin a dissection, you're working with pieces and parts. The frog is the living, jumping animal you see in your terrarium. Once you cut into it, you're no longer dealing with the real, whole frog—just frog parts."

She set down the frog and the dissection and walked around the desk. "Don't get me wrong. Dissections are important for education and research. It's a valuable tool to increase our understanding of an organism and even to develop ways to improve the lives of these animals and our own lives. However, it's important that you never confuse frog parts with a living frog. Once you cut into the frog, you can never put it back together. The whole is always more than just the sum of its parts."

In the same way, sometimes we get so caught up in the parts of the Wellness Concept that we forget people don't actually exist in parts. We may gain a better understanding by doing a conceptual dissection of a person, but in the real world, we don't live dissected lives. We live as complex, whole persons that any model falls short of explaining completely. When we try to use Wellness Theory to guide programs, teaching, and ministry, we often take one area at a time and try to offer something that will encourage growth in that one area. That's okay, but there are some dangers with this approach as well. One is that when we address people as parts, we also tend to encourage them to segment their lives. The parts don't seem to impact each other. A student in an English class can write a brilliant essay on plagiarism and not cite any sources. A leader in your church can cheat on his taxes.

While working as a lead counselor for Indian Village at Forest Home Christian Conference Center, I once led a group of elementary school kids in a game of Capture the Flag[93] against the other village. The contest was filled with the usual rule-bending, arguing, and outright cheating. As we walked back after the game, I found myself at the end of the line with a boy who did his own share of cheating.

[93] The game where everyone cheats, no one wins, and someone usually gets hurt.

He turned to me and asked, "Bear[94], are all the non-Christians in the other village? They sure did cheat a lot."

[94] "Bear" is my "Indian" name. Thousands of kids know me only as Bear, and some of my former staff can't call me anything else.

He associated not cheating with being a Christian, but he couldn't connect not cheating with playing the game. He'd learned these things separately, so they never connected in his life.

Figure 10
Prism Model

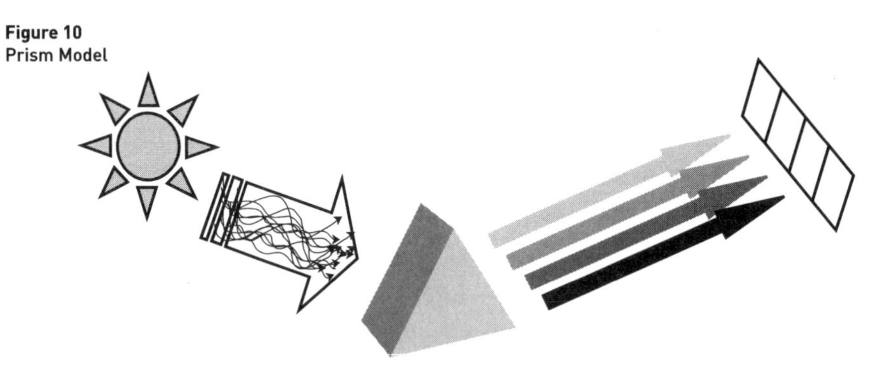

Let me offer another wellness model. Picture a prism (figure 10). A prism refracts light.[95] Light from a source like the sun or a flame is sent through a prism and separated into a spectrum. Light on the front side of the prism is a tangle of many different wavelengths of light. They all mix together so we see a single color. The prism separates these wavelengths so each component wave can be seen as a distinct color on the other side. Each light source creates a unique spectrum with different amounts of color, separated at different places. We learn much about the source of the light by the spectrum a prism creates. But the spectrum isn't the source; the spectrum the sun produces isn't the sun. We gain understanding on one side of the prism, but we live on the other side.

[95] "To refract light" basically means to bend the light so it separates into individual wavelengths. I wanted to use a big word so you'd think I learned more in college than just how to cut things up.

Like the prism, Wellness divides people into component parts so we can better understand them. While we can use this information for better understanding, we also need to create programs and learning opportunities that can be used on the front side of the prism—in real life. Physical, social, intellectual, spiritual, and emotional areas mix together like the wavelengths of sunlight on the front side of the prism. The Wellness Concept, like a prism, helps us identify, understand, and address the unique needs in each area.

Wellness becomes a powerful tool for us as leaders and teachers as we use it to create opportunities for each area to touch, interact, and inform all the other areas. With this, wellness becomes a way to wholeness and a way for us to work toward presenting people perfect and complete in Christ.

Implications and Applications

Wellness and wholeness are very useful concepts while working with individuals. We can use them to identify areas where a student may be struggling and accurately offer support. We can also identify where a student is comfortable and challenge her to grow in that area.[96] Understanding the different parts of a person can also give us "entry points," the areas where a person enjoys focusing—a person's preferred area.

For example, some people feel very comfortable playing sports and being physical, while others prefer a more social context. An entry point gives us access to areas in a person's life that may be more difficult for them to deal with or discuss. Some of the guys I work with are very comfortable in the physical aspect of their lives. Thus, some of my most intimate and powerful ministry happens while shooting baskets or playing catch. If I were to directly ask these young men about their walks with God or about their relationships with their parents, I'd get a one-word answer every time: "Good."[97] But as we toss a football back and forth, I meet them in a "safe place" where they feel confident and comfortable (being physically active), thus allowing them to more easily explore areas where they feel less confident or where they're struggling. If we take the time to discover a person's entry point, we gain access to the pain and challenges she faces in other areas of her life, and then we can accurately offer advice and support.[98]

The Wellness Concept also offers insight into how we can love and support teenagers in crisis or transition.[99] Often there's nothing we can do to take away the challenges they face. In fact, we may steal their opportunities for growth if we do. Instead, we can help them deal with the challenging areas by offering support in other areas. If a student is facing a huge test or project,[100] we can't do the project for him; however, we ***can*** take the pressure off in other areas: e.g., help him complete chores around home,[101] study with him instead of just hang out,[102] pray with and for him.[103] As he's supported in these other areas, he'll have more time and energy to devote to the area of challenge.

Wellness can give us great insights into how we can communicate with people, and how we can accurately challenge and support them. Wholeness encourages us to consider how we can help people connect and integrate all aspects of their lives. As leaders and teachers, these concepts offer ways to promote powerful growth. As pastors and ministers, Wellness and Wholeness not only give us insight into how a person lives, but also give us permission to impact the entire sphere of a person's life.

[96] See "Dynamics of Growth"—Comfort Zones.

[97] If I catch them at an unusually vulnerable moment, I might get "'S all good."

[98] I explore entry points in more depth when I lead facilitation-training programs through Praxis Training.

[99] Of course you must know your limits. If a person is in crisis, referring her to a counselor should always be a primary way to support her.

[100] This is an example of a challenge in the Intellectual area of Wellness.

[101] A way you can offer support in the Physical and Social areas.

[102] More support in the Social area, as well as the Intellectual area.

[103] Spiritual support.

Section Two

ACTIVITIES AND EXERCISES

ACTIVITIES AND EXERCISES[104]

This section contains **Activity Briefs**—short summaries or notes about useful activities and exercises. They can be used to create artificial situations that allow participants to be themselves, notice how they feel and what they do, and try out new ways of dealing with experiences. **These activities work best when used in light of and in conjunction with the theories and models offered in the first section of this book.** The following isn't an exhaustive or even complete list of activities or instructions.

[104] Welcome to the Activities Section! If you only bought this book as an addition to your "Games Library," I hope you'll eventually read the other parts of the book as well. If not, then please read this introduction.

These briefs assume you've had some training in leading activities. If you want to get the full power from these activities, you'll need to be intentional about using them experientially. Whenever you use them, the way you introduce them, where they're done, and how you sequence them are just a few of the factors that will impact the outcome. You can also do these activities and exercises just for fun; but they'll lose some of their power, and you'll miss out on opportunities to change lives.

The Disclaimer

While I've done my best to offer these activities so you can use them in a safe and instructive way, I acknowledge there are limits as to how effectively a book format carries this out. These activities are wonderful, powerful tools that I believe can truly increase your effectiveness as a guide, facilitator, pastor, leader, and teacher. However, I'd be making a huge mistake if I didn't inform you of the risks you take in applying this material. That's what this disclaimer is about:

> *Experiential activities and exercises can present elements of physical, emotional, and interpersonal risk. Whenever you, as a leader, use these activities, you must ultimately assume the responsibility for judging their suitability and safety. This book is intended to be a reference source only. The author and publisher assume no liability or responsibility for how the information in this book is used or applied. This includes errors or accidents due to omission of details, misprints, or typographical errors.*
>
> *Neither this book, nor any book, can replace practical experience, training, and education. The intent of this material is to introduce the idea of experiential*

methods in the context of youth ministry. You're strongly encouraged to seek additional training and experience as you implement these concepts.

Enjoy and be safe!

The Activities

The activities in this section are presented in a way to make them user friendly and encourage depth. Each is divided into as many as six parts.

Activity Brief

This is a short explanation of the activity and some ideas about how to present it. You're encouraged to "make it yours" and use your creativity to enhance the activity. You may notice that the titles and briefs for some of these activities hint at a story or scenario I use. Use these stories or create new ones that better fit the group you're working with. Be creative, but remember—you're responsible for the changes you make. Be sure the changes enhance the activity and don't distract from the learning or the fun.

Equipment

While some of the activities require no equipment other than space to play and your imagination, others require simple everyday objects, and still others require specialized equipment or access to a challenge course. Where specialized equipment and locations are required, I've tried to offer suggestions or alternatives.

Safety

Your judgment and decision-making ability are the most important factors in keeping your students and leaders safe. In this section I offer some insights into safety concerns for the activity. In the end, it's your responsibility to create the safest learning environment possible. You need to understand "actual risk" versus "perceived risk."

Consider This

Since the point of this book is to learn how to use experiences intentionally, teaching this section offers insight into common issues and lessons that typically come up during the activity. Don't limit yourself to the topics listed. Use your observation skills and personal judgment to look for additional topics and insights that arise from your group's experiences.

Variations

With minor changes, each activity can be presented and used in a different way. This section offers variations I've used for the activity. Usually it involves a change or addition of props or a slight spin on the rules or activity brief.

Personal Notes and Re-View

You're encouraged to write your own observations and variations in the space provided. As you lead an activity, you'll gain insight into how it works best for you. Record these ideas so you can adapt and change the activity to ultimately make it your own.

Important!

I wish I could give proper credit to the creator of each of these activities. Most of the activities I use I either learned long ago from a source that is blurred in my memory, adapted from activities I've used in the past, or they're a result of a "spur of the moment"[105] idea or opportunity. In reality, there are few, if any, original activities or exercises in this book. However, many either have twists or use different props that make them unique to me or to the people I've trained.

[105] Read: a moment of panic or a time when I found myself unprepared and had to grab a prop off the wall and just make something up.

Even if I can't identify an activity's origins, I still must acknowledge that it wasn't written or created in a vacuum. If there is anything new in this book, it's only because I stand on the shoulders of giant rubber chickens that have come before me.[106] Listed in the appendix are what I consider to be some of the best and most complete books, Web sites, and conferences for activities and experiential methods. I must acknowledge a few people who greatly influenced my choice of activities; most are either direct knockoffs or somehow derived from something Karl Rohnke has written or done at some point in his extensive career.

[106] A poor reference to Abe Lincoln's famous quotation—"If I see any farther, it is because I stand on the shoulders of giants."

For the last 10 years, Jim Cain and Chris Cavert have written, coauthored, or somehow been involved in the best resources out there. Tom Leahy hosts the National Challenge Course Practitioners Symposium every February in Boulder, Colorado. He manages to gather the most creative and energetic group of experiential professionals from all over the world. Everyone is welcome, and this creates an amazingly powerful conference where I never cease to be challenged and fed.

Many of my ideas and activities have been created and tested as I've worked in college student leadership development with Andre Coleman, Danny Mann, Katie Fischer, and Priscilla Losey for the last several years. Their input and insights have been invaluable in my personal growth and in the writing of this book. While my name is on the cover, these people—along with all the groups and facilitators I've worked with up to this point—have impacted and influenced me. They should get most of the credit[107] (and none of the blame) for Section 2 of this book.

[107] In a very real, yet nonlegal and nonfinancial way.

INITIATIVE ACTIVITIES (25 OF THEM)

Chapter 2.1

Initiative activities are exercises that involve groups[108] of people in situations with specific limitations and real consequences. They create situations where participants are challenged in many different areas of Wellness,[109] and they move people out of their comfort zones.[110] These activities should be considered starting points—a place to move from, not a place to stop.

You can use these activities as they're written in this book. If you do, I'm sure you'll discover new and better ways to do them. As you improve these activities and make them your own, be sure you write down your discoveries in the Personal Notes and Re-View section.[111] I'd love to hear how you use these activities as well.[112]

[108] Usually group initiatives involve as few as two people and as many as 25. I like working with groups of 10 to 14 for most of the activities listed in this section.

[109] See the "Spheres of Growth" section.

[110] See the "Dynamics of Growth" section.

[111] Write in this book. If you didn't read the Introduction, go back and see why I encourage people to write in books.

[112] E-mail me your changes and adaptations: BearLosey@sbcglobal.net.

1. Bucket Lift

If you're looking for an excuse to get your group wet, here's a great activity for a smaller group on a hot day. There's a lot of flexibility in how you lead this activity and what kind of container is used. Whatever you choose, this activity requires cooperation from everyone and offers real consequences for any lapse in concentration.

1. Fill a five-gallon bucket[113] to the top with water and have the group sit around it.
2. Challenge the group to lift the bucket off the ground—using only their feet–without spilling a drop.
3. Once they've lifted the bucket, challenge them to take off their shoes without setting the container down and without spilling any water. Each person must have at least one foot on the bucket at all times.
4. Challenge them to other creative tasks.

[113] Any kind of bucket large enough for your whole group to sit around and put their feet on will work. The key considerations are that there's room for your whole group and that the bucket isn't too heavy when it's filled with water. An industrial-size oil drum might be too big.

Equipment

All you need is a five-gallon bucket (or other container), water source, and an open area that can survive getting wet.

Safety

Before you do this activity, you may want to check to see if anyone in the group has back problems or other conditions that may make lying on the ground and lifting heavy objects unsafe. A safe water container is also important. Be sure there are no sharp edges or places where socks or skin might get snagged. Wire bucket handles can be a hazard and they should be removed.

Consider This

This activity can either show how well a team can work together or reveal their limitations. Does the group take any time to plan this challenge? The simple instructions can sometimes lead the group to think the task is easy. How does the group react when you ask them to take off their shoes or do some other task without first setting down the bucket?

One person or a small portion of the group can "hijack" this activity and end up dumping the water on someone. This might be a sign of discord or of a power play going on in the group. "But we were just having fun!" might be their excuse, but does the "we" they talk about include everyone?

Variations

In order to create a little variety and change the challenge a bit, you might try putting something other than water in the bucket. Changing the size and shape of the bucket can be interesting too. A smaller bucket changes the challenge to finding a place for all the feet, while a square bucket can increase the difficulty of moving or spinning it.

Personal Notes and Re-View

2. The Grid[114] (a.k.a. The Maze or Gridlock)

There is a difference between solving a problem and being "in" the problem. Participants get to experience both roles during this activity as they deal with trial-and-error problem solving and stepping into the unknown.

1. Lay out a grid on the ground (you can use chalk, tape, tiles, or whatever[115]). The size of the grid can vary with the size of your group. The larger the grid, the more challenging the activity. (I suggest at least eight feet by eight feet; 10 feet by 10 feet works as well.)
2. Create a path through the grid and record it on a piece of paper. Graph paper makes creating the solution very easy. Don't mark the actual grid. Keep the paper with the solution to yourself. The path doesn't need to go from one side to the opposite. You can make it as convoluted as you want.
3. When it's time to do the activity, inform the group (using any story that fits—traffic gridlock, "Indiana Jones," or just an unknown maze) there's a one-way path through the maze. Only one person at a time is allowed in the maze, but they will all need to go through it. The person in the maze continues as long as they stay on the path. If they step off the path, then they must leave the maze and the next person can begin trying to discover the path. (It's fun to sound a buzzer or some sort of similar audio effect whenever a person steps off the path.)
4. Everyone in the group must attempt the grid before anyone can try it a second time.
5. The activity ends when the complete path is discovered and everyone in the group has gone through the grid.

Hints:

- Don't let them mark the path.
- The path is a sequence of moves. They may step on a square that is part of the path during one move, but then miss the square on their **next** step. That's still a wrong move, so that person has stepped off the path and must leave the maze. One way to communicate this idea to the group is to let them know that once they've discovered a new part of the path, all the squares surrounding that one are now possible moves once again.
- Give them only negative information. In other words, buzz them when they make an incorrect move, but say nothing when they make a correct move.

IMPORTANT—As a facilitator you'll need to pay close attention to every move and keep track of the moves on the "solution paper" you made before the activity.

[114] Jim Cain and Barry Jolliff's *Teamwork and Teamplay* (Kendall/Hunt Publishing Company, 1998) has a great version of this activity called "Gridlock."

[115] You can purchase grids from equipment suppliers such as www.praxistraining.com and www.Teamworkandteamplay.com and others. You can also make your own prefab grid with a tarp and either tape or spray paint.

Equipment

You'll need tape, chalk, or some other way of creating a grid, solution paper (graph paper with the correct path marked on it), and some sort of noisemaking device to let the maze walkers know when they make a wrong step.

Safety

There are few physical safety issues in this activity. Social and emotional safety may become issues as the participants' frustration increases.

Consider This

Did the group develop a system? How did they decide which directions to try? How did people outside the grid help the person inside? How was advice given?

Personal Notes and Re-View

3. Inside Out/Outside In

This simple activity will get your group thinking about how they work together.

1. Use a rope, webbing, or cord to create a large circle on the ground (large enough for the whole team to stand in with little difficulty).
2. Start off with a fun story about the group being held in a dungeon or a sci-fi force field container.
3. Ask the group to stand inside the circle.
4. The challenge is to have the whole group get out of the circle without using or allowing the rope to touch any parts of their arms (from the shoulder on down). In other words, if they use their hands, elbows, or shoulders in any way, then their whole group needs to start over.
5. Once they're all outside the circle, have them repeat the challenge from the outside and go back in the same way they came out.

Equipment

All that's needed is some sort of floor marker that can be lifted. A rope, string, webbing, or even the group's shoestrings can work.

Safety

While most groups will keep this activity pretty low-key and safe, some groups may find ways to challenge the safety boundaries by trying to jump, dive, or otherwise fling their bodies under the rope. This should be discouraged.

Consider This

Some groups will solve this activity in just minutes, but they'll discover the real challenge is executing their plan. Does solving the problem intellectually mean completing the task? How many times do they attempt a strategy before giving up? Other groups may struggle to find a solution due to "overthinking" the task. As the facilitator, it can be both highly entertaining and extremely frustrating to watch the group wrestle with issues that only exist in their shared misunderstanding of the task. What rules are they assuming exist that aren't really there? How were these rules introduced?

Variations

Increase the intensity of this activity by asking the group to put their hands either in their pockets or hold them behind their backs. The activity also changes when you use different types of line to create the "dungeon"; a very light line, like ribbon or kite string, behaves very differently from static line or even an extension cord.

Personal Notes and Re-View

4. Proton Transfer (a.k.a. Marble Tubes)

Your group may not have realized they'd be working with radioactive materials such as protons.[116] These "protons" are very radioactive and require special equipment to move them—the Proton Transfer Apparatus.[117] Once you receive the transport tubes, you must move the five protons from their current locations to the radioactive waste depository[118] using only the tubes.

[116] Marbles.

[117] They may look like 90-degree molding cut into one-foot pieces (or PVC tubes cut the same), but they're really highly technical pieces of equipment.

[118] A paper cup or Tupperware container.

1. Place the radioactive waste depository at least 20 yards away from the bag of protons. The bag of protons is the starting point.
2. Have each member of the group grab one length of tube.
3. The proton must pass through all the tubes before it can pass through any tube a second time.
4. At no time may your skin touch the protons.
5. Participants cannot move their feet if there is a proton in their tube.
6. If any proton is dropped, anything other than a tube touches the proton, or anyone moves a foot when there's a proton in the tube, the group (or just the proton) must start over again.

Equipment

I have two types of marble tubes. I use PVC pipes (½- to ¾-inch—make sure your marbles fit) with holes large enough so a marble can fall out midtube if a person's not careful. The most cost-effective and easiest tubes to make are just pieces of corner molding (they look like 10-foot long Scrabble tile racks) cut into approximately one-foot lengths. You'll also need marbles. They can be bought by the bag at most toy stores or sometimes you can find "decorative" marbles at garden stores or specialty shops. The last piece of equipment you'll need is some sort of receptacle. A coffee cup or paper drinking cup work well, but I've had to improvise an ending point many times. (Coiled webbing or string, a soup can, and a hollow depression in a rock have all worked well.)

Safety

The biggest safety risk for this activity is usually a result of frustration or fatigue. When some proton mover teams get frustrated, they may use the marble tubes as weapons. Others, when not engaged in the activity, may get distracted and the tubes will somehow become imaginary swords or knives. Still other groups may take the concept of "passing" the protons a bit too literally and use the tubes to fling marbles at the next person. This kind of play can become a real safety issue.[119]

[119] Those memorable words of caution that Ralphie heard repeatedly in *A Christmas Story* (MGM/UA, 1983) come to mind: "You'll shoot your eye out!"

Consider This

This can be a very difficult activity, and it will challenge the group to perform at a high level.[120] How does the group create and agree to a plan? How many different

[120] One group I worked with called this "The game they play in hell."

strategies did the group try? How many times did they attempt a strategy before they abandoned it? Did they abandon a plan because it was a poor plan or because of poor execution? Was maintaining focus a problem? What happened when individuals lost focus?

Variations

Changing the size of the marble and the distance to the "depository" will impact the level of difficulty. In order to eliminate the possibility of some overly creative solutions, yet increase the challenge, you might want to add a rule: The marble can only touch one tube at a time.

Personal Notes and Re-View

5. Mousetrap Gauntlet[121]

Mousetraps are a great prop that can be used in multiple ways. This is the first challenge I experienced using these devices. It's a challenge of trust and communication with real consequences.

[121] Many thanks to Sam Sikes for the mousetrap activities. He's a wealth of creativity and wisdom in the world of experiential training. Check out www.DoingWorks.com.

1. Create a large circle on the floor with rope or some other marker.
2. Have each member of the group grab two or three unset mousetraps and a bandana.
3. Teach them how to safely handle and set the traps.
4. Have them set their traps and carefully place them on the ground in the circle.
5. As the facilitator, you can also set a few more traps in the circle to fill in any open spaces.
6. Have the group pair off; the twosomes should separate and stand on opposite sides of the circle.
7. At this point ask them to take off their shoes (and also their socks, if they don't want to get them dirty).
8. One member of each pair will put on a bandana as a blindfold. His partner will then guide him through the circle of mousetraps—with only his voice.

9. Have all the pairs go at the same time.
10. Once one person in the pair has gone through the circle, have them switch places.
11. Once both have completed this task, have them find new buddies and go again.

Equipment

You'll need 50 or more mousetraps, one blindfold for each pair, and rope (or something to mark the circle).

Safety

Be sure to use small mousetraps and not rat traps. The mousetraps will pinch and may, at worst, create a red mark if they snap someone; but they won't do any real damage. Extra caution and care should be used whenever you ask people to wear blindfolds.

Consider This

It's amazing how much anxiety these mousetraps can create in some people. How do individuals respond when they're standing in the middle of a circle full of traps? How do they respond when they're guiding a partner? How does the anxiety vary between people? This activity also emphasizes the importance of clarity in communication. How does the communication change as the activity progresses?

Variations

Repeat the task but without using words. The guides can make only sounds but no words that you'd find in a dictionary. Another variation would be to have them get into groups of three. One team member walks through the circle blindfolded. The second person isn't blindfolded, so he watches and whispers instructions to the third person on the team who *is* blindfolded, but is also allowed to speak out loud and warn or guide the blindfolded person inside the circle.

Personal Notes and Re-View

6. Mousetrap Tower

Extreme Jenga! The challenge to this activity is to build a tower as tall as possible using loaded mousetraps.

1. Gather the group around a steady table or other flat, stable workspace. Have at least 20 unset mousetraps spread out on the surface.
2. Challenge the group to create a freestanding structure using only set mousetraps. This structure needs to be as tall as possible and needs to be completed in 10 minutes.

Equipment

You'll need at least 20 mousetraps and room to build.

Safety

Be sure to use small mousetraps rather than the larger rat traps. The small traps are scary but inflict minimal pain or injury.[122]

[122] Of course poor judgment can make any prop a lethal weapon. Mousetraps can become very dangerous. As fun or funny as it may seem, don't let people intentionally snap any body parts in the traps. There are also sharp wire ends that can poke and puncture if the mousetrap is thrown, kicked, or otherwise becomes a projectile.

Consider This

Performing under stressful conditions becomes a major theme in this activity. How do people respond to being asked to act when the consequences are immediate and obvious? How do individuals handle failure? How does the group treat the person who is placing a trap when the tower falls?

Variations

When you switch the emphasis from working as a group to working as individuals, this activity changes dramatically. Another interesting variation is to have them first build a tower with unset mousetraps and then build another tower with the traps set. How does that change the process?

Personal Notes and Re-View

7. Floor Sensors (Mucus River Crossing)

This classic activity can be introduced with many different scenarios. However, "Floor Sensors" is a fun spy story that engages the group's imagination.

1. Your group receives special pads,[123] one per person, which will allow them to defeat the floor sensors in order to reach their objective (the other side of a room) (figure 11).
2. Once they're handed out, these pads must remain in direct contact with a person at all times or else they'll deactivate and be lost forever. That means the facilitator—you—can take a pad away whenever you see that a player has lost contact with it.
3. The pads will activate the sensors if they slide across the floor, so they must be picked up and repositioned each time they're used.
4. Your entire team must cross the room without activating the floor sensors.
5. The only way across is by using the pads.

[123] Pads can be carpet squares, paper plates, bandanas, or any marker large enough to stand on.

Figure 11
Floor Sensors

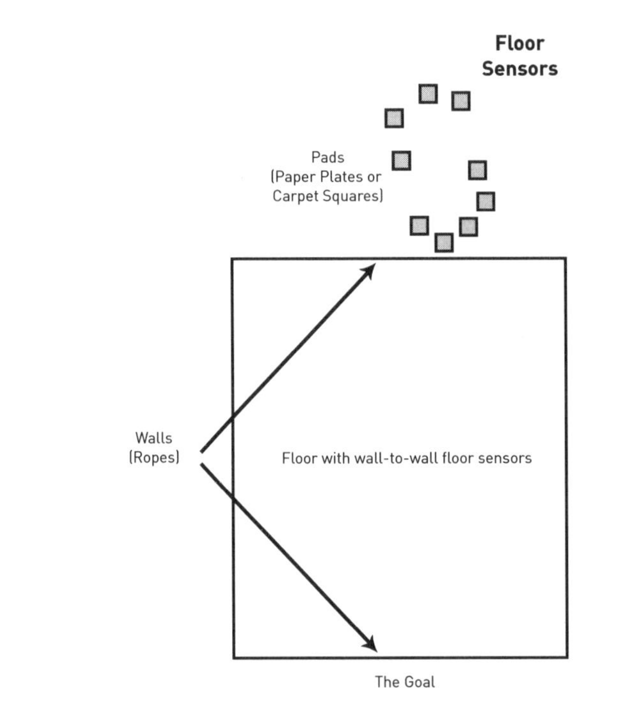

Equipment

You'll need pads. I commonly use paper plates but also have a bunch of carpet samples that can be used as well. You'll also need some way of creating a starting point and an ending point or goal. Two ropes work, but with the floor sensor scenario, you can use a room with doors at both ends.

Safety

There are a few safety issues to watch for in this activity. Before you start, check to be sure the pads don't easily slide on the surface of the floor. If they slide too easily, then a participant may fall when moving from pad to pad. As pads are lost, the group will need to have more than one person cross over on a pad. Unless you have enough spotters, don't allow them to stack up on each other's shoulders. Keep an eye on how far apart they place the pads. Even the most secure pad will slide if a person is leaping onto it from a long distance. This may seem like common sense, but you should also let the players know there is no headfirst diving allowed.

Consider This

This activity offers plenty of opportunities for failure. When someone drops a pad and it's lost, how does the rest of the group respond? How does the person who lost it react? What are the group's reactions and feelings when someone steps on the floor and the whole group has to start over? The group often discovers it can complete the task with far fewer resources than first imagined. Look for those breakthrough moments. Solutions typically involve close physical proximity. How do different people respond to this closeness?

Variations

The size of the pads changes the difficulty level of this activity. Carpet samples can easily hold two or three people, while small paper plates or napkins create a more difficult problem to overcome. Instead of making the whole group start over when someone touches the floor, just have that one person go back or give that player some awkward object to carry the rest of the way.

Personal Notes and Re-View

8. Reach Out

The groups will find that they can reach much farther than they think. This activity will help them see and use resources they've always had but never noticed.

1. Create a "home base." Players can't be away from the home base unless they're still connected to someone who's inside or touching the base.
2. The goal is to reach as far from the base as possible, while always staying physically connected to home base.
3. If anyone becomes disconnected from the group, and therefore the home base, the whole group must return to the base and start over.

Hints: Let them discover what "connected" means. They may use anything they have to stay connected (belts, jackets, shoe strings, and so on). Lay out a goal that ***seems*** impossible but really is possible if they discover the resources and use them.

Equipment

The only thing you need is an open field or large gym to play in.

Safety

Check the playing surface (especially if you're playing outside) to be sure there are no holes, sharp objects, or other hazards. Also watch for issues regarding social appropriateness.[124]

[124] I was once working with an all-female group who took off their bras to reach farther.

Consider This

It's always fun to see how a group reacts when you ask them to do something they believe is impossible. What are some of their initial comments about the challenge? When asked to use personal items to extend the group's reach, how do different people respond? How does the group talk about being connected?

Variations

Place resources (such as a broomstick, short rope, tree branches, and so on) out on the field that the group members can pick up and use along the way to extend their reach even farther.

Personal Notes and Re-View

9. The Road to Community (Indiana Jones Crossing)

The group will find this activity very challenging if they don't plan carefully or pay attention to details. Making the easy choice early on can make the task impossible later.

1. Using paper plates or other markers, create a pattern similar to the one below (figure 12).
2. The whole group must cross the "gap" by only stepping on the plates.
3. All the plates are available. However, once a plate is "fully weighted" (with a person on it, not just a rock or a shoe), it must ***stay*** fully weighted or else it disintegrates (the facilitator takes it away).

Figure 12
The Road to Community

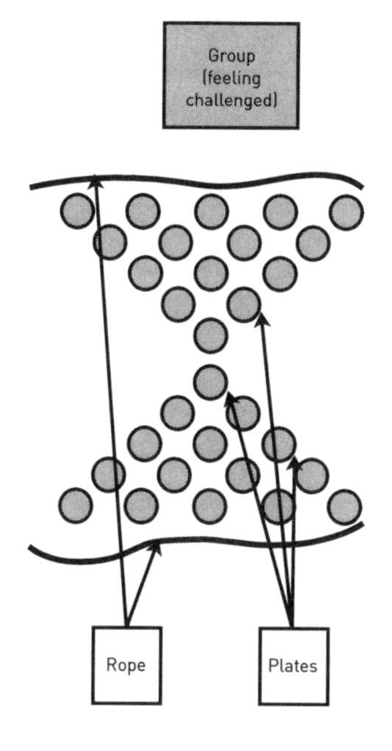

Equipment

Paper plates, bandanas, carpet squares, or any other item a person can safely stand on will work as a marker. You'll also need some sort of lines (rope, tape, or preexisting markers) to create the boundaries.

Safety

Leaping and jumping can become safety issues as markers are removed and the gap between steps increases. Be sure the markers don't slide easily and don't allow headfirst diving.

Consider This

With just a bit of planning, this activity can be completed quickly and easily. How do the actions of the first people to get across impact those who cross later? How does the group respond when key markers are removed? When a group doesn't carefully plan the first few crossings, the first members to go may have an easy time of it, but then the options become limited for the last part of the group. What happens when focus is lost?

Variations

The degree of challenge can be increased or decreased based on the number and placement of the markers. If the group completes the task easily, ask them to go back using only the remaining markers. You can also ask them to see how many times they can cross before there aren't enough markers left for the whole group to make the return trip.

Personal Notes and Re-View

[125] I know this activity is outlined in several other books, but I learned to love this activity after playing it with Chris Cavert.

10. Rope Star[125]

This is a fun way to energize a group and get them problem solving and moving together.

1. Tie a long rope into a circle.
2. Have the group grab onto the rope, and they should be evenly distributed all the way around.
3. The first part of this challenge is for the group to form a five-pointed star (the way you learned to draw a star back in elementary school) without letting go of the rope (figure 13).
4. After they've created the star, have them reverse the procedure to get back into a circle.
5. Now challenge the group to see how quickly they can create the star again.

Equipment

A long length of rope and an open space.

Figure 13
Rope Star

Safety

As the group becomes more confident, they'll begin to move quickly while stepping over and under the rope. Make sure they watch for tripping or "clotheslining"[126] hazards. If you let them slide their hands along the rope, be sure to warn them about the potential for rope burns.

[126] "Clotheslining" is when a person runs into a rope at neck level and his legs fly out from under him. It's very painful and not very fun.

Consider This

It may take them awhile to figure out how to move together to make the star at first. What are some of the major turning points in their process? How do their actions and movements change with each attempt? Compare the first attempt to the last attempt. How much time did it take for each? How did the movements change? What is different about their communication?

Variations

Using a different length of rope can offer different levels of challenge. The number of people holding onto the rope can create different experiences as well.

Personal Notes and Re-View

11. Through the Card

Did you ever cut paper into snowflakes as a child? This challenge looks impossible; but with a bit of creativity, it is very possible (figure 14).

1. Each member of the group is given a 3x5 card and access to scissors.
2. The challenge is to create a hole in a 3x5 card large enough for the entire group to fit through.
3. The card cannot be taped, glued, or otherwise reattached. The group cannot rip the card as it passes through the hole.

Figure 14 Through the Card

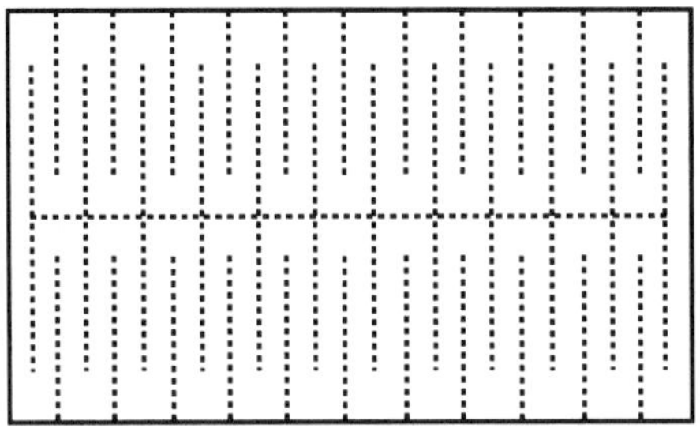

This is one way to cut the card. Fold the card in half lengthwise. Start the cut on the folded side and make alternating cuts that stop before you reach the other side. Then make one big cut along the fold, except for the first and last folds. (Don't reveal this solution until your kids have completely given up.)

Equipment

All you need are 3x5 cards and scissors.

Safety

The usual precautions of working with sharp objects should be taken.

Consider This

The group is asked to complete a seemingly impossible task. What is their initial reaction to the challenge? What do they say? Do they discuss the problem and possible solutions? Do they ever despair over completing the task?

Variations

Give the group a letter-sized sheet of paper and challenge them to create a hole they can drive a car through. Allow some time for the group to consider the problem individually, but then let them work together as a group.

Personal Notes and Re-View

12. Toxic Waste[127]

This activity can be done by one group or you can have multiple groups working on this problem at the same time.

[127] I've seen many variations on this activity. Al Wright added the food color aspect.

Scenario:

Say—**You're a team of toxic materials specialists. Some materials have been discovered and isolated** (figure 15) **but the danger is grave. Within the next 30 minutes, you must neutralize the chemicals. Your job is to figure out how to turn all liquid toxic wastes to an equal shade of green. Any neutralization exercises must occur within the inner circle of the neutralizer transfer zone. Green toxic waste must then be returned to the original contamination circle. Any direct human contact with the toxic materials or their containers will mean the loss of limbs or other physical resources for that individual. Any human occupying a space closer than 12 feet from the cans is a case of clear contamination. No drops of the waste must be spilled without a team penalty. Possible penalties include having to start over or losing a team leader.**

Figure 15
Toxic Waste

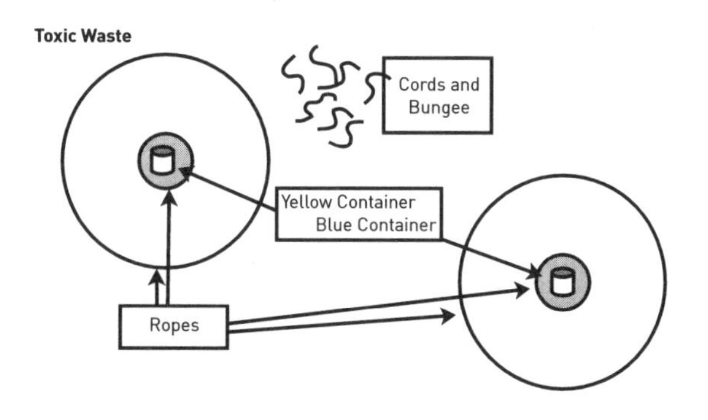

Equipment

This activity requires a complex setup and briefing. You need ropes to create the outer boundaries and ropes for the inner circles as well. Paint cans or other buckets work well for the containers. Both containers should be filled with water. One will have blue food coloring, the other yellow food coloring. Eight to 15 lengths of string should be laid out for each group, along with a length of shock or bungee cord.

Safety

Overstressing the shock cord may create snapback issues.

Consider This

The first challenge is for the group to figure out what color their toxic waste is. Then they have to figure out how to change the color. How much time do they spend trying to solve the problem without gaining all the information they need first? This activity also allows people with different abilities and specialized knowledge to shine. How does the team discover these key people? How do they use others in the group? Do any group members "buy-out"? If so, why?

Variations

I've seen this activity done with as many as six different groups. No single group can complete this activity on their own, so it creates the need to redefine who's in your group. It also creates opportunities for negotiation and different ideas about competition versus cooperation.

Personal Notes and Re-View

13. Collection of Knots

This is a simple, low-prop activity that is fun and encourages closeness and communication.

1. Lay out a rope that is long enough for the whole group to hold onto with one hand and with one to two yards between them.
2. Ask the group to pick up the rope. Each person can only have one hand on the rope and they must be spread out evenly.
3. The challenge is to have the group create a simple overhand knot between each person in the group. No slip knots or loops.
4. They cannot let go or otherwise move the hands that are holding the rope.

Equipment

You'll need one long rope.

Safety

Any rough pulling or yanking can become dangerous and should be discouraged. Give the group permission to let go of the rope before any wrenching or limb twisting occurs.

Consider This

The solution requires movement and cooperation. How do they come up with a plan? Do they just work at one spot or work from both ends of the rope? Does everyone understand the plan when they start to use it? What are the people who are away from the action doing and saying?

Variations

Groups who understand knots can be challenged to tie figure-eight knots between each person instead. You can also challenge them to undo the knots after they've completed the task. Another variation is to have the group tie just one square knot around a tree or pole.

Personal Notes and Re-View

14. Blind Maze

The intensity of this activity may surprise people. It's amazing how difficult it can be for some people to ask for help.

1. Set up a rope path that creates a circuit—a "maze" that has no entry and no exit (figure 16).
2. Gather the group at a spot out of sight from the maze so they can't see it ahead of time.
3. Inform them that you're going to lead them—blindfolded—into a rope maze. Their task is to get out of the maze.
4. They may only talk to the facilitator. They cannot talk to anyone else.
5. Have the group put blindfolds over their eyes and hold the hands or shoulders of their teammates. Then lead them to the maze.

6. Place all the individuals next to the rope and have them grab onto it. Tell them they must hold onto the rope until they're told otherwise. Remind them that the rope is the maze, they need to get out of the maze, and they can only talk to the facilitator. Tell them not to start until they're told to do so.
7. After the whole group has been positioned in the maze, tell them they may begin to find their way out of the maze.
8. The only way out is to ask for help. Talk to individuals and answer their questions, but don't take them out of the maze until they specifically ask you for help. Once a person asks for help, lead her away from the rope, remove her blindfold, and have her sit quietly. Group members who are removed from the maze before the activity ends may not speak to anyone in the maze or offer assistance in any way.

Figure 16
Blind Maze

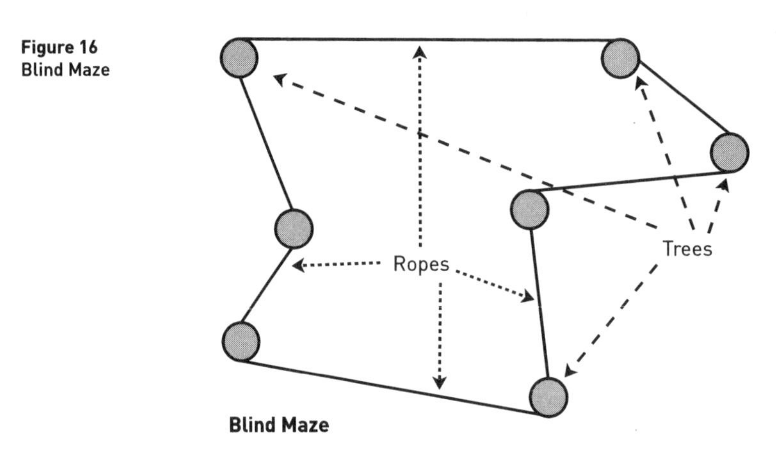

Equipment

You'll need enough rope to make a large maze, and one blindfold for each person.

Safety

Whenever you limit visibility or work with blindfolds you should exercise caution and use your best judgment. Walk slowly as you lead the group, and keep an eye on the end of the line. Be observant as you set up the rope maze. Watch out for tripping hazards, low branches, and other obstacles that could cause a person to fall or accidentally run into solid or pointy objects.

Consider This

This maze isn't solved by conventional thinking. How do people react when they realize the rope is a circuit? How do they handle not being able to speak to each other? Who has the hardest time admitting they need help? What keeps them from asking for help?

Variations

The feeling of isolation increases as you create longer distances between turns in the maze. Out in the middle, a person feels exposed and lonely. You may choose to allow the maze walkers to speak to each other. This often increases their frustration, and they also tend to lash out at the facilitator more.

Personal Notes and Re-View

15. Find My Keys!

A simple and all-too-real scenario can become a great group challenge that requires planning, clear communication, and cooperation.

1. Out of sight from the group, place a key somewhere in a large, grassy field.[128] Be sure to make a map of the field and record where you place the key.
2. Lead the group to the edge of the field, and tell them a key that opens the lock to a safe containing the cure to cancer[129] is lost someplace in the field. The safe will self-destruct in 20 minutes. They must find the key before time runs out.

Equipment

A large field and a key[130] are all you need.

Safety

Be sure to check the field for tripping and other hazards before the activity. Also be sure there are no animal or insect issues.[131]

Consider This

If the field is large enough, there will be no way for them to find the key during the time limit without an organized search. How much time do they spend planning?

[128] The field should be large enough so the group can't form a single line that is as long as any one side of the field. A good rule for the size of the field is to have at least 15 feet between each person on any one side. For a group of 10, that would mean a field at least 150-feet long.

[129] Or some other wonderful treasure or desired object.

[130] I don't recommend using a key to any important door or valued automobile. Even though you record where you place the key, it may never be found.

[131] I've witnessed the overnight appearance of a beehive near a field I'd used many times.

How does the group manage the tension between organizing the search and the time limit? If they do take time to plan, how many options are presented? How many ideas are considered? How is a decision reached?

Variations

The degree of challenge for this activity is directly related to the size of the search area and the time allowed to search. Changing the search objective from a key to a person can increase the urgency. Another fun alternative is to only allow the group to talk when they're off the field. If they're in the search area, they must remain silent.

Personal Notes and Re-View

16. Putty Golf

This can be a fun way to get a group moving around, laughing, and concentrating as well.

1. Clear out a large space in a room. Mark a large circle with rope or tape, and place a hole[132] in the center.
2. Give each group member a hunk[133] of Silly Putty.
3. The challenge is to have the putty bounce into the "hole." First on only one bounce, then after two bounces, and so on. Players must toss the putty from outside the boundary line for the attempt to count. The goal is to see how many times you can get the putty to bounce before it goes into the hole.

[132] An empty trash can or coffee can works well.

[133] Your definition of "hunk" will probably be determined by how much Silly Putty you have. In my mind a "hunk" is about the size of a golf ball.

Equipment

You'll need enough Silly Putty[134] for the group, plus a can or other receptacle to serve as the hole. You can use a rope for the boundary line, or you can require players to be touching a wall when they toss the putty.

[134] There are several places online where you can buy Silly Putty in bulk. I use www.funstuffusa.com. (They also offer great deals on Pez dispensers.)

Safety

Tossing Silly Putty is pretty safe. When the toss becomes a throw, however, the putty turns into a projectile and can do great damage to both persons and property.[135] Continue to remind the group to toss rather than throw the putty. After the toss, they'll also have to retrieve the putty before their next turn. This means there'll be much laughter during the chasing of the putty. Encourage the group to be careful during the chase.

[135] I know this from experience.

Consider This

For the most part, this activity is all about laughter and motion. However, you may be able to get a read on which group members are more competitive. Watch to see if they help each other out by retrieving putty balls or if they ignore all putty but their own. Do they celebrate only when they make a hole or do they celebrate with others? How much do they talk about winning versus individual accomplishment?

Variations

Silly Putty is fun to use, but you can use super balls or ping pong balls as well. This activity can also be super sized and played outside using large playground balls and garbage cans.

Personal Notes and Re-View

17. Orienteering

Not too many people know how to use a compass these days. This activity requires players to learn a new skill and apply it right away.

1. Before the activity begins, lay out an orienteering course with at least three legs: a starting point, initial direction, and distance (for example, 30 degrees for 40 yards). At that location, place three markers—one on the correct location and two others just a little off.
2. Lay out the second leg starting from that location with a new direction and distance. Place three more markers—again, one on the correct spot and two others nearby.
3. Create a third leg the same way.
4. When the group arrives, give them some instructions on compass use—how to get their bearings and how to follow a course. Also teach them how to measure their pacing. Lay out a 50-foot rope and have them walk it at least three times while counting their steps. Take the average number of paces and divide it by 50 feet. That will give them a pretty accurate measurement of the length of each person's pace.
5. Have them get into teams of three people. Give each team a compass and a paper containing the location information.
6. The challenge is for each team to find the final location by correctly walking all three legs of the course.
7. If they don't correctly identify the final location, they must start all over.

Equipment

You'll need one compass for every three people in the group. You'll also need one compass for yourself and a way to measure the distances between locations. I have a 50-foot length of cord that I've marked off in one-foot intervals. For markers I use very small sticks or screws in grassy areas and bits of masking tape on hard surfaces.

Safety

Be sure to avoid tripping hazards as you mark off the course. Be sure there is no way a team can mistakenly wander onto a busy street or other dangerous location.

Consider This

Consistency and concentration are essential for success in this activity. Mistakes and miscalculations are amplified. Detailed and patient people are rewarded. How carefully do they use their compasses? Does the same person do the pacing each time? How do they divide the tasks?

Variations

To increase the difficulty you can place more location markers at each leg or—even more difficult—not place any markers at all. They must do all three legs without any feedback. To make this a bit easier you can give them one set of directions/distances at a time. Once they find the right location, give them the next set.

Personal Notes and Re-View

18. Amoeba Walk

The group will be challenged to work together in very close quarters.

1. Tie a rope into a circle large enough for the whole group to squeeze into. Make sure they can all fit but not too comfortably.
2. Give the rope to the group and ask them all to step inside it.
3. Now challenge the group to a game of follow the leader. While following you around the room, the whole group must stay inside the rope. The rope must also stay off the ground, and they cannot touch the rope with any part of their hands or arms.
4. Lead the group through an increasingly difficult obstacle course. Just walking will be difficult at first. As the group adjusts, lead them up and down stairs, under or over handrails, and through other interesting challenges.

Equipment

All you need is some sort of rope or line just large enough for the group to squeeze into.

Safety

Lead slowly. Keep an eye on the group and be sure you're listening to both the front and back of the circle. Be aware of the surface you're leading them over. The group can watch out for its members; but if it isn't, then you can call for a safety stop and remind them that they need to care for each other.

Consider This

The Amoeba Walk creates a different experience depending on where you find yourself in the circle. What's it like to be in front? In back? In the middle? How did the task change as you did the different obstacles? What helped the amoeba move well? What held it back?

Variations

Smaller or larger lengths of rope change the dynamics of this activity. You can increase the intensity by creating an "eye spot"—blindfold all but one or two people in the amoeba.

Personal Notes and Re-View

19. Bucket Brigade

You may have played this as a relay race at a camp or on a picnic. With a simple briefing, it turns into a great group challenge.

1. Give the group enough paper plates for each person to have one.
2. Show them a water source and an empty five-gallon bucket positioned about 20 yards apart.
3. The group must fill the bucket to overflowing as quickly as possible and using the only resource they have on them.

Equipment

You'll need enough paper plates for the group, a five-gallon bucket, and some sort of water source (such as a new, large trash can filled with water).

Safety

Water can make any surface slippery. Encourage the group to use caution while they're running. Be sure the location you choose is free of all tripping hazards. And for health reasons, no water may be transported inside anyone's mouth.

Consider This

This activity relies on communication, cooperation, and especially creativity. Does the group identify and use any resources other than the paper plates? How do they use the flat plates to transport water? As the activity progresses, how do they deal with the changing nature (soggy state) of the plates?

Variations

Of course the size of the containers and the distance between the water source and the bucket will impact the level of challenge for this activity. Instead of paper plates, you may want to give the group several different objects: a few plates, a few small cups, duct tape, and so on. If you really want to get creative, you can challenge them to move Jell-O instead of water.

Personal Notes and Re-View

[136] I found this activity in *Teambuilding Puzzles* by Anderson, Cain, Cavert, and Heck (FUNdoing Publications, 2005). Not only does it contain great pictures of the solution to this challenge, but it also has great puzzles, activities, and revealing essays that offer great insights into experiential learning.

20. Leonardo's Bridge[136]

This is a very technical challenge for smaller groups. It's based in history, and the design is truly functional.

1. Give the group the materials to build a freestanding bridge.
2. The challenge is to construct a bridge using only the given materials. The bridge must be freestanding and it must be able to support whatever weight the group is given during the testing phase.

Equipment

The bridge-building kit contains fifteen dowels. Ten larger diameter dowels have three notches cut into them (figure 17). Five smaller diameter dowels have no notches. Either a large book, such as a dictionary, or several Bibles can be used to test how much weight the bridge can support.

Figure 17
Special Bridge Dowel

Safety

The major safety consideration for this activity is the misuse of the materials whenever the group members' frustration levels increase. As the group struggles, the dowels may turn into weapons or projectiles. This should be avoided.

Consider This

This is an activity with one intended solution. The bridge-building kit is based on a design created by Leonardo da Vinci. As the bridge is built, it depends on its own weight for stability. How does the group go about exploring the use of the dowels? Does anyone in the group have special knowledge or engineering skills? How are individual talents and limitations expressed and explored?

Variations

A large bridge-building kit can be made and used to create a bridge strong enough for a person to use to cross over an obstacle. (This test must be done with spotters.) A bridge kit based on Roman arch designs can also be created. It consists of rectangular blocks that must be fit together with a keystone.

Personal Notes and Re-View

21. Blindfolded Tent Building

If you're camping and have time to do group development, then this is the activity for you. You may want to use a spare tent though.

1. Show the group a tent already set up or a picture of an assembled tent.
2. The challenge is for the group to set up an identical tent—while they're blindfolded. All the parts will be laid out for them to look at—but not touch—for one minute before they're blindfolded.
3. The challenge is finished when everyone in the group agrees that the tent is up.

Equipment

You'll need a tent that has several parts. The more parts there are, the more challenging this activity becomes. You'll also need to have another tent or at least have a large picture of a tent that is already set up.

Safety

Safety is always an issue when people are blindfolded. Choose an area to do this activity that is clear of low branches and tripping hazards. Keep a close eye on all participants, and be sure to catch them before they get too close to a hazard. Be watchful as long tent poles are moved around so they don't poke or smack[137] any participants. Some people may be not like being blindfolded. Offer the option of closing their eyes, but stress the need for integrity.

[137] Technically known as a "Three Stooges Incident."

Consider This

Some people have trouble setting up tents even when their eyes are uncovered. How does the group compensate for the loss of their vision? Do they spend any time organizing before they jump right into the construction? How is a plan decided upon? How is leadership decided upon?

Variations

The style and complexity of the tent will impact the level of challenge. You can also allow one person to see but not talk to the group. Or perhaps the sighted guide is only allowed to ***whisper*** instructions to the others.

Personal Notes and Re-View

22. Blueprints

The importance of clear and precise communication is highlighted by this activity.

1. Divide the group into two teams.
2. Place the teams in separate rooms or far enough away from each other so they can't hear or see what the other team is doing.
3. Give each team a set of blocks that has the exact same number, size, and color of pieces.
4. Their challenge is to build a structure using all the blocks and then create blueprints for the other team to recreate an exact duplicate of the structure. They have 20 minutes to create both the structure and the blueprints.
5. After 20 minutes, exchange the blueprints and give the teams 10 minutes to build an exact duplicate of the other team's structure.

Equipment

You'll need at least two sets of blocks. LEGO bricks, Lincoln Logs, or plain wooden blocks work well. There are all kinds of other building toys that will work too. Each group will also need paper and pencils to create the blueprints.

Safety

With any increase in frustration, the blocks may become projectiles. This should be discouraged.

Consider This

Different people require different levels of detail. How much detail is enough? Does the blueprint list the color of each block? How does the group adjust its plans to meet the different levels of precision? How do they divide the labors of construction and creation of the plans?

Variations

The size, shape, and complexity of the block sets used will impact how difficult and detailed the blueprints will need to be. Using basic wooden blocks creates limited options, while using an erector set opens up all sorts of new design directions. You can decide whether or not the group can include pictures in their blueprints or use only words to describe how to build the structure.

Personal Notes and Re-View

23. In the Bucket

This is a timed event. The group will need to look at a problem in new and different ways as they try to cut their time.

1. Place a large, clean trash can or barrel in the middle of a room or open area.
2. Spread 60–100 tennis balls around the room.
3. Challenge the group to see how quickly they can get all the balls into the barrel.
4. Each person must touch at least three tennis balls before they go into the barrel.
5. They'll have as many attempts as they'd like in order to try different strategies and improve their time.

Equipment

You'll need a whole bunch of tennis balls[138, 139] and a barrel. One of the things that makes this challenge work is the size of the barrel. It must be large enough to fit all the balls, but not so big that the whole group can stand around it at the same time.

[138] You'll need at least five or six balls for each person.

[139] Check with a country club or tennis team and ask if they'll donate old tennis balls.

Safety

Safety decreases if tossing becomes throwing. Also be aware of "bonking" as people crowd around the barrel.

Consider This

Be sure to record the time of each attempt. How much time do they spend discussing a plan before they start their first attempt? What do they discover after the first attempt? After later attempts? How many times do they try a strategy before they abandon it? How quickly do they think they can accomplish the task after their first attempt? Are they surprised by their final time?

Variations

If tennis balls are a limited resource in your area, you can do this activity with a variety of objects. Even a bunch of different things can be used, as long as they can all fit into the container. The key to making this activity challenging is to use a large number of objects the group cannot carry all at once.

Personal Notes and Re-View

24. Group Karaoke

If you have a karaoke machine or some musical talent in your group, this activity will create hysterical video opportunities.

1. Ask the group to agree on a karaoke song they can sing together.[140]
2. Once they agree on a song, inform them they'll have to sing it together. Not all at the same time, but one word at a time.
3. Each person can only sing one word, and they each take turns singing into the microphone. Everyone must sing a word before anyone else can sing a second time. If they skip a person, miss a word, or fall behind in the song, then they must start over.
4. The challenge is finished when they've completed the first verse and the chorus.[141]

[140] This part may be just as challenging as the actual activity.

[141] Doing the entire song may be too sadistic and evil.

Equipment

A karaoke machine[142] works best, but you can also use a truly sadistic musician, if you know any, who won't slow the song's tempo—no matter what.

[142] Karaoke machines are pretty cheap at discount stores.

Safety

Limiting the amount of the song to be sung will help limit the chance of insanity caused by hearing the same bad rendition of a song done over and over and over.

Consider This

There will be much laughter and fun at the start of this activity. When and why does it stop being fun for everyone? What is the real challenge of this activity? How does the group handle the different tolerance levels for messing around? How did their song choice impact the level of challenge? Would they choose a different song if they knew ahead of time how they'd have to sing it? What do they think of that song now?

Variations

Adding one or two microphones will decrease the level of challenge.

Personal Notes and Re-View

25. Song Timer

This isn't so much an activity as it is a way to add some fun to any activity that requires the group to perform for a set amount of time. If they need to hold a position for a minute or build something that must stand for 30 seconds, this is a fun way to track the time without using a stopwatch. If the challenge requires a time limit (between 30 seconds and a few minutes long) or a specific amount of time to complete a task, ask the group to choose a song they can all sing together. Do this before you introduce the activity so they can't guess what the song might be for. Once they agree on the song, have them practice it together one time. Compliment them on how beautiful they sound, and then introduce the activity. Tell them they must do whatever the activity requires for the amount of time it takes them to sing the song. If they don't finish the challenge or somehow fall short before the song is finished, then they must start over.

Consider This

They usually sing the song at a moderate tempo to start. How does the song change as the activity progresses? Does anyone resist changing the song? Why? How does their understanding of the role of the song change as the activity progresses? Did their song choice impact the level of challenge of the activity?

Personal Notes and Re-View

EXERCISES FOR SMALL GROUPS
(11 OF THEM)

Chapter 2.2

These exercises and activities are intended for small groups[143] and tend to be less physically active than initiative activities. They create great opportunities for individual reflection and group conversation. Look over the "Consider This" section, but look and listen for other interesting reactions and topics that may arise as a result of these activities.

[143] Fewer than 10 people.

Again you're encouraged to make them your own. Be sure to write down your observations and variations in the "Personal Notes and Re-View" sections and, in all your free time, send me an e-mail to tell me about your creative revisions and applications.

1. Clips and Cards

This activity reveals how a group approaches a project from start to completion.

1. Have the group split into teams of four or five people.
2. Give each group a pack of 3x5 index cards and a box of 100 paper clips.
3. Tell them they have 10 minutes to build the tallest freestanding structure possible using only the clips and the cards they've been given.

Equipment

You'll need one pack of index cards and one box of paper clips for each team.

Consider This

There are several designs that work well for this activity. How do they decide on a design and a strategy? Who leads? Does the leader role transfer to others? How do they divide roles and tasks? How do they manage their time?

Variations
If they don't use all the clips or cards, have the teams repeat the activity using only those resources they used to make the first structure. Challenge them to build a taller structure this time.

Personal Notes and Re-View

2. Creative Lies
This is a fun "get to know you" activity that encourages creativity and listening skills.

1. Have participants get into groups of three.
2. In each group, Person #1 will deliver a two-minute autobiography to Person #2. Person #2 should listen carefully to Person #1.
3. Then Person #2 is to create an extended biography—a positive, creative story—about what Person #1 will do and accomplish during the next five years.
4. Person #2 now has two minutes to tell Person #3 the creative lie about Person #1's future.
5. Repeat this process for each person in the group: Person #3 makes up a creative lie for Person #2, Person #1 creates a creative lie for Person #3, and so on.

Equipment
Nothing is needed for this activity.

Consider This
While this is a fun "get to know you" activity, it also reveals listening skills and the ability to connect with a person's goals and direction in life. What did people like about the lie that was told about them? What didn't they like? How well did the lie connect to the actual history of the person? Did they think the creative lie was positive?

Variations

A simple way to create variations for this activity is to change the format of the creative lie. Have them do an episode of ***E! True Hollywood Story***, a Biography Channel special, or even a ***National Enquirer*** report.

Personal Notes and Re-View

3. Personal Web Page

This project can help the group get to know each other in a creative way. It also creates a tool that will allow them to explore personal connections during breaks in the action.

1. Before the group arrives, spread out flip chart paper, pens, magazines, and other resources on different tables or work stations.
2. As people arrive instruct them to take a few minutes to create their own personal "Web pages."
3. On a sheet of paper, they should design a one-page introduction of themselves that can be posted on the wall.
4. Tell them their pages should include:

   - Their names
   - Where they're from
   - What organization(s) they work with
   - Why they're here
   - Favorite room in the house and why
   - Personal theme songs
   - Self-portraits
   - One question they have
   - One answer they have
   - Anything else they think the group should know

5. When they're finished creating, have each one give a two-minute overview of their creations. Encourage everyone to "surf" the posted Web pages during the breaks in your meeting time.

Equipment

At the very least you'll need enough poster paper or flip chart paper for everyone in the group to make a Web page, colored pens, and tape. You may also want to provide magazines, scissors, and glue sticks for them to cut out and attach a few pictures. Other art supplies can also be fun to include.

Consider This

This is an opportunity to observe the group and pick up some indicators of learning styles and personality preferences. How detailed do they get? Does this become a sticking point or an obstacle? How clear is their vision for the page? Do they ask for specific colors or other materials? Or do they explore what's available? If you look for behaviors and choices like these, then your observations may offer some clues about the different types of people you have in your group.

Variations

The format and the specific questions can be adapted to fit your unique situation. You can let them be creative with interpreting technology by adding hyperlinks, downloads, blogs, or "flash" animations.[144]

[144] I have no clue how they'd add these things, but I've ceased to be surprised at the creativity of people.

Personal Notes and Re-View

4. What Is This?

Gather some common objects and expand your group's imagination and creativity. I use this activity to help people see ordinary things in new and different ways.

1. Collect four or five common objects small enough to be passed around.
2. Gather the group around you and hold up one of the objects. Ask them, "What is this?" After they give the obvious answer, tell them they'll each have to answer that same question as the object is passed around the group, but they cannot use an answer that's already been given. For example, if you hold up a water bottle, then no one can use "water bottle" as an answer to "What is this?" The next person might say, "It's plastic." Now no one else can use ***that*** answer. When it's their turn, they must come up with original and creative responses.
3. After everyone provides an answer for the first object, hold up another object, ask, "What is this?" and then pass it around in the other direction.

Equipment

You can either gather some fun objects before you begin the activity, or you can just randomly grab things from around the room. Be sure the objects aren't too delicate and that you have permission to handle them.

Consider This

Some people will find this activity easier than others. What makes this activity a challenge? Which objects were easy and which were more difficult? Why? What was the most creative answer? How did this activity change the way you look at things?

Variations

Change the question from "What is this?" to "What can you do with this?" and you have a whole new activity.

Personal Notes and Re-View

5. And Then...But Before That...

Getting everyone in a group to participate in a debriefing discussion can be a challenge. This tool encourages everyone to contribute, and it also creates a group memory of whatever event you wish to debrief.

1. Gather the group together and have them take a few minutes to reflect on the event or activity to be debriefed.
2. Tell them they're going to work together to reconstruct the event—step by step.
3. Each person will take a turn telling what happened and in the sequence they remember it.
4. The first person tells how the event began (how they remember it, anyway). Remind the group members to keep it short. In three or four sentences, they should describe a portion of the activity.
5. Then the next person starts with one of two phrases.[145] They can either say, "And then...," and continue describing the event from where the last person stopped, or they can say, "But before that...," if they feel something was left out of the reconstruction of the event.
6. Continue going around the group until the whole event has been relived.

[145] You can also offer a third option: Allow a player to pass to the next person.

Equipment

Nothing is needed for this activity.

Consider This

Listen carefully to the "But before that..." portions of the discussion. These will reveal what that person thinks is significant. Are there any parts of the event the whole group skips or ignores? Are there any disagreements as to the sequence of actual events?

Variations

This activity offers one format that you can use for group storytelling. But you can also do a variation called "Tag Out." This version offers a "tag-team" wrestling approach. One person begins to recount the events of the activity. When they want to stop, they reach out a hand and say, "Tag out." Another person then touches the storyteller's hand and begins where that person stopped. Other members of the group can hold out their hands to let the person who's talking know they wish to be tagged in.

Personal Notes and Re-View

6. "Once Upon a Time..."

This is a great activity to try while sitting around camp, or if you don't want to watch TV or a movie.

1. Have everyone in the group write down three characters on a slip of paper. For example, a cow, a mushroom, and the king of England. On a separate piece of paper, have them write a setting or location. For example, a sailboat.
2. Collect the slips of paper and put all the characters into one bowl or hat and the settings into another container.
3. Have a volunteer take a slip from each container and read them silently.
4. Then she begins the story by saying, for example, "Once upon a time there was a cow, a mushroom, and the king of England on a sailboat." (The person should insert whatever characters and setting were drawn from the container.)
5. The person sitting next to her must then pick up the story and add a few sentences to the plot.
6. Each person takes a turn telling the next part of the story until everyone has contributed.
7. The person who started the story goes last, and she must also create an ending to the story.
8. Another volunteer then picks a new slip from each container, and the group repeats the process.

Equipment

You just need slips of paper and something to write with for all the participants, plus two containers to hold the slips of paper.

Consider This

You don't have to go through all the slips of paper, but you might want to do three or four rounds. Do you notice any common themes among all the stories? Do some people use the same or similar events or plot twists in their parts of the story?

Variations

For the creatively advanced, you don't need to do the slips of paper—just jump into "Once upon a time..." and let their imaginations run. Instead of having each person contribute only once, you can let the story continue until it reaches a natural end.

Personal Notes and Re-View

7. The Inbox

People see the world differently. This simple prioritization exercise creates an opportunity for people to reveal what's important to them.

1. Make copies of **The Inbox** worksheet **(page 93)**, one for each person.
2. Hand out copies to the group, and tell them they have 15 minutes to decide what to do with the items listed on the sheet. They should work individually.
3. Now have them get into pairs. Give them another 15 minutes to work together and come to a consensus on how to handle the inbox items.
4. Finally, divide them into groups of six or eight and give these new groups another 15 minutes to come up with a single group strategy for dealing with the inbox.

Equipment

Copies of **The Inbox** worksheet **(page 93)** and something to write with for each person.

Consider This

As more people have input regarding how to handle the items in the inbox, the task gets more difficult. How did they make their decisions when they worked on the sheet individually? How did they decide what to do as groups of two or more? Did they ever, as a group, talk about how they made decisions?

Variations

The Inbox worksheet is a generic list of schedule items and to-dos. You may want to use the same worksheet format, but create your own list of things, based on the unique group you work with.

Personal Notes and Re-View

The Inbox

It's Monday morning. You turn on your computer and find the following information in your day planner. Everything has to be addressed by Friday afternoon. Below is an inbox filled with tasks, assignments, meetings, and other to-do items. There are also three priority boxes: "Urgent," "Needs to Get Done," and "Not Gonna Happen." You need to decide in which priority box each item belongs. You have 15 minutes to complete this worksheet.

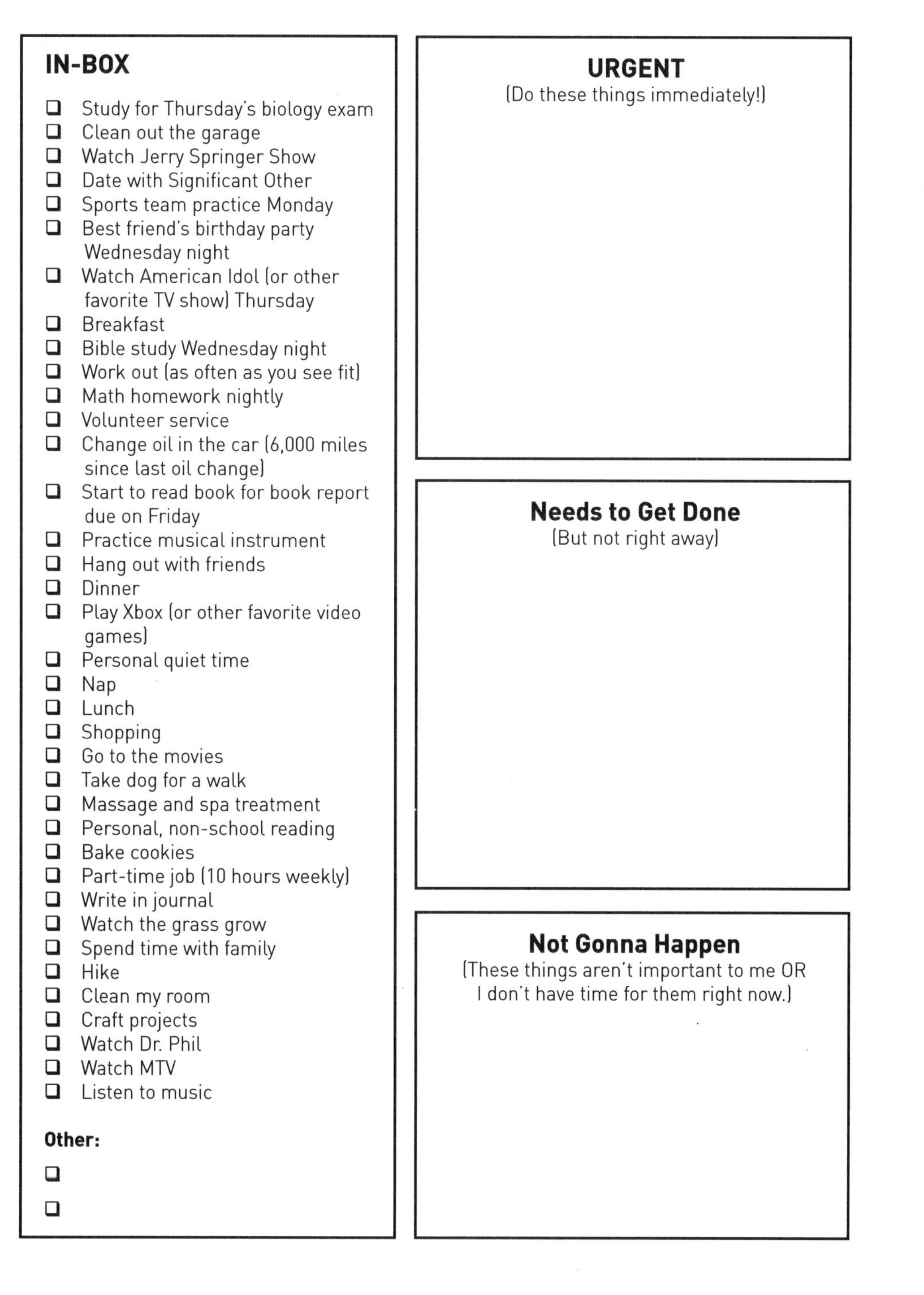

IN-BOX

- ❑ Study for Thursday's biology exam
- ❑ Clean out the garage
- ❑ Watch Jerry Springer Show
- ❑ Date with Significant Other
- ❑ Sports team practice Monday
- ❑ Best friend's birthday party Wednesday night
- ❑ Watch American Idol (or other favorite TV show) Thursday
- ❑ Breakfast
- ❑ Bible study Wednesday night
- ❑ Work out (as often as you see fit)
- ❑ Math homework nightly
- ❑ Volunteer service
- ❑ Change oil in the car (6,000 miles since last oil change)
- ❑ Start to read book for book report due on Friday
- ❑ Practice musical instrument
- ❑ Hang out with friends
- ❑ Dinner
- ❑ Play Xbox (or other favorite video games)
- ❑ Personal quiet time
- ❑ Nap
- ❑ Lunch
- ❑ Shopping
- ❑ Go to the movies
- ❑ Take dog for a walk
- ❑ Massage and spa treatment
- ❑ Personal, non-school reading
- ❑ Bake cookies
- ❑ Part-time job (10 hours weekly)
- ❑ Write in journal
- ❑ Watch the grass grow
- ❑ Spend time with family
- ❑ Hike
- ❑ Clean my room
- ❑ Craft projects
- ❑ Watch Dr. Phil
- ❑ Watch MTV
- ❑ Listen to music

Other:

- ❑
- ❑

URGENT

(Do these things immediately!)

Needs to Get Done

(But not right away)

Not Gonna Happen

(These things aren't important to me OR I don't have time for them right now.)

8. Karaoke Sharing

If you have access to a karaoke machine, this is a fun way for people to describe how they're doing or what they're feeling.

1. Hand out a list of available songs for your karaoke machine to each person in the group.
2. Give them 10 minutes to reflect on the activity or event while looking over the song list. Ask them to choose one or two songs that describe their attitudes or feelings.
3. Gather the group around the sound system.
4. Ask a few volunteers to share or sing their selections.
5. Ask those who don't want to sing to just share the song titles they chose.

Equipment

You need a simple karaoke machine and copies of the list of available songs.

Consider This

It's important to remember that people will respond very differently to this activity. Some will love the creative challenge and the performance required with this type of sharing, while others will be terrified by these very same elements. Notice how each member of the group responds to this exercise.

Variations

You can do this without a karaoke system. Just create your own list of songs for the group to use.

Personal Notes and Re-View

9. Nail Stacking[146]

With very simple supplies, you can create a great individual or group puzzle.

1. Set out a bunch of large nails and a small block of wood.
2. Challenge the group to see how many nails they can balance or stack onto one single nail that's placed point down on the block of wood.

[146] *Teambuilding Puzzles* by Anderson, Cain, Cavert, and Heck (FUNdoing Publications, 2005) has a great write-up on this activity. It also provides the solution and some variations.

Equipment

This puzzle consists of 15 or more nails and a small block of wood. The wood block needs to have a small hole that a nail will fit into snugly.

Consider This

This is an intellectual challenge when completed by individuals, but the interpersonal challenge soon becomes the major obstacle once more people try to work together to solve this puzzle. Watch and listen for how ideas are shared and explored. How do they determine when to try an idea? When to abandon an idea? How are failure and frustration dealt with?

Variations

You can build large versions of this activity with tent spikes or even longer dowels. Another variation is to set two bases (blocks of wood) two or more feet apart[147] and then challenge the group to find a way to make a bridge between two nails stuck in the bases.[148]

[147] The distance just needs to be longer than any nail you're using.

[148] This is one of those "paradigm shifters" that really frustrates people. The best way to make the bridge is to move the bases closer together.

Personal Notes and Re-View

[149] Thanks to Shari Bunn for this activity.

[150] For more theater and improvisation activities, look at *Theatre Games and Beyond* by Amiel Schotz (Meriwether Publishing, Ltd., 1998) and *Improvisation, Inc.* by Robert Lowe (Pfeiffer, 2000).

10. Rain of Grace[149]

Drama activities are a great way to challenge a group to share their feelings and emotions.[150] This isn't an activity for a group of strangers. If the group has been together for a while and trusts each other, this can be a wonderful way to let go of some things that are stressful.

1. Give the group several minutes to reflect silently on the things that are currently stressing them out or weighing them down.
2. Have the group self-select into groups of three.
3. Ask for a volunteer to start.
4. The volunteer stands between the two other people in his triad and shares what is stressing him out. He then chooses one word that represents that stressful situation and closes his eyes.
5. The other two people will represent that stress by saying the word over and over again while GENTLY poking and pushing the volunteer for about 30 seconds.
6. After about 30 seconds of GENTLE pushing, poking, and repetition of the stress word, the two stressors change. They stop harassing and softly move their hands up and down the arms of the volunteer while softly saying "Grace" over and over again. They should "rain grace" on the person for about 20 seconds.
7. Allow a few moments of silence before moving on to the next person.
8. Do this for each person in the group.

Equipment

Nothing is needed for this activity.

Safety

If the group isn't ready for this level of sharing and vulnerability, or if it's not taking the exercise seriously, this activity can create an emotionally hazardous situation. The "touching" aspect might make participants uncomfortable, so be sure to encourage them to take it seriously. There may be some nervous laughter, but get them to see what's beyond that.

Consider This

Most people aren't used to having their stress spoken out loud and physically manifested. How do they feel as they're "pushed" by their stressors? What's it like when they switch to grace? What's it like to be the stressor? How do we play these roles in our everyday lives?

Variations

Instead of doing this activity in groups of three, consider doing it in slightly larger groups. You could even do it as a "fishbowl" exercise, where a triad volunteers to do this activity in front of a larger group. Afterward the entire group discusses what took place during the exercise from the three different perspectives, specifically noting changes in the participants' body positioning and language.

Personal Notes and Re-View

11. "Tilly Miller"

This is a classic riddle that creates a division in the group: Those who get it and those who don't.

1. Start by saying, "Did you know Tilly Miller likes the moon but doesn't like stars?"
2. Ask if anyone knows what else Tilly Miller likes or doesn't like.
3. If they say they do, then they must make a statement about what Tilly likes or doesn't like. (For example, Tilly likes grass but not the lawn, floors but not rugs.)
4. Some people may already know this riddle; others will be able to figure it out quickly.
5. Don't offer the solution. Let people wrestle with it.
6. After a while move on to a discussion or another riddle to solve.

Solution:[151] The main clue is in the name Ti**ll**y Mi**ll**er. Tilly only likes words containing double letters.

[151] Riddles are supposed to be wrestled with, so offering the solution here goes against my personal riddle ethics. But I'm willing to compromise for you.

Equipment

Nothing is needed for this activity.

Consider This

Riddles create an "in-group" and an "out-group" based on who figures out the solution and who doesn't. What's it like when you hear a riddle you already know? What about when you hear a riddle you've heard before but can't remember the solution? Describe how you feel when you figure out the solution on your own. How does it feel to watch others figure out the solution while you're still wrestling with the riddle?

Variations

There are many riddles that can be used besides "Tilly Miller." Use your favorite riddles to explore the issues involved with inclusion and exclusion. "Crossed/ Uncrossed," "Counting Sticks," and "She Died," just to name a few.

Personal Notes and Re-View

LARGE GROUP ACTIVITIES
(9 OF THEM)

Chapter 2.3

You may find yourself working with large groups of people.[152] While some of these activities can be done with smaller groups, they work best with lots of people. The idea is to engage all the people for the duration of the activity. Most leaders don't expect much learning to come from large group mixers or icebreakers, but the following activities can be led in a way that not only helps people connect to others, but also offers lessons about themselves.

[152] I consider a large group to consist of anywhere between 30 and 500 people, depending on the location, context, and goals of the event.

1. Braveheart

Fun and loud!

1. Have the group line up single file along the edge of a field (or a wall) and face the open ground.
2. Share with them about the scene from the movie ***Braveheart*** where the soldiers are lined up and waiting to charge into battle. When they're told to advance, they begin to yell and charge forward.
3. Tell the group they're now like those soldiers, and they're about to charge into battle.
4. The challenge is that as they charge forward, they must scream as loud as they can, but they can only use one breath. Also, they must walk heel touching toe—one foot right in front of the other. Once they run out of breath, they must stop walking and stand wherever they stopped.
5. Do this a few times and see if they can go any farther each time.

Hint: This can either be just for fun or you might have them imagine some sort of challenge that faces them in the future.

Equipment

A very large field or activity room is needed for this activity.

Consider This

Allow time for laughter, but also watch the group. Ask them a few things, such as "How was each attempt different?" and "Why do you tend to go farther with each attempt?" If you gave them something to focus on, ask them how having that perspective impacted the experience.

Variations

Instead of walking forward, you can challenge the group to walk backward heel to toe, crab walk, or bear crawl.

Personal Notes and Re-View

2. Find Your Herd

This activity takes a small amount of preparation, but it's a fun way to start a day of activities and to divide people into groups—either intentionally or randomly.

1. Write the names of different animals on 3x5 cards (one animal on each card, one card for each person). There should only be one animal assigned to each group. So if you have five groups, then you'd use the names of five different animals.
2. Explain to the group that this is a role-playing game. In a moment they'll receive their roles written on cards. Once they receive their cards, they need to quietly wait for further instructions. (No sharing their assigned animals ahead of time.)
3. Pass out the cards.
4. Tell the group they must now find their "herds" by role-playing the animals on their cards. They can only make animal noises and actions.
5. Once a group is sure the herd is complete, it should introduce itself to the rest of the herds.

Equipment

You'll need to make a set of animal cards. Decide how many groups you'd like to create, and then choose an animal for each group. If you want to select group membership intentionally, you can use a roster of participants to create nametags or cards with the animal group name written on the back of each card or tag.

Consider This

This activity involves some role-playing. How much do people get into their characters? Is this more challenging for some than for others? In what ways do they interpret the animals differently? Do these variations affect how well they find each other?

Variations

Animals create some fun role-playing opportunities, but other subjects work as well: movies or television shows (or characters from these), countries, rock stars, and so on.

Personal Notes and Re-View

3. House Sitting

This is just a fun excuse to run around and join people together.

1. Have the participants get into groups of three.
2. Have two of them (the house) stand facing each other with their arms raised and their hands touching above the head of the third person (the tenant).
3. When the leader calls out "Eviction!" all the tenants must leave their houses and find another house to occupy. The house (both people) remains where it is, hoping a new tenant will arrive.
4. When the leader calls out "Demolition!" the houses (both people creating the house) must leave and create a new house with a new person as their tenant. In this instance, the tenant stands still and waits for a new house to form over him.
5. When the leader calls out "Earthquake!" all of the participants must create new houses with new tenants. Encourage lots of yelling and screaming and simulated panic.

Hint: You can make this an elimination event by giving players a limited amount of time to find a new house or tenant, or you can just let the group have fun and run around.

Equipment

A large playing field or activity room is all that's needed for this activity.

Consider This

While this activity is intended to be fun, loud, and wild, it can also be a big challenge for people who are either unfamiliar with the group or just aren't comfortable acting as wild as the others. You can get some idea of a group's—or certain individuals'—willingness to participate during activities that are "just fun."

Variations

Using your imagination, you can use any structure, animal, or situation that can be broken down into three or more components and turn it into this joining-in-the-fun activity. What might it look like for groups of three to make an ***elephant*** instead of a house? And what different things might you call out?

Personal Notes and Re-View

4. That Person Over There[153]

This is a large-group activity that breaks down barriers and creates connections.

[153] Thanks again to Chris Cavert for this one.

1. Begin by introducing yourself to anyone in the group. Learn the person's name and maybe something about her. Be sure to pay attention to what she says and what she looks like.
2. Next, move on to someone else and introduce yourself to him.
3. After you introduce yourself, locate the first person you met, point to her, and say to the second person, "That person over there is..." and say her name and what you learned about her.
4. Now learn this new person's name and information.
5. Go to a third person, introduce yourself, and say, "That person over there is..." while pointing to the last person you talked to. Then say, "And that person over there is ..." while pointing to the first person you met.
6. Repeat this and see how many different people you can string together and say, "That person over there..."

Equipment

Nothing is needed for this activity.

Consider This

While this activity will be easy for the outgoing people in the group, it may be a challenge for others who are more shy or introverted. Watch for people who aren't engaged in the activity. And for some people, this is just the excuse they need to interact with some new people. At the very least, they'll learn a few new names.

Variations

Try Tom's Two-Minute Frenzy **(page 109)**.

Personal Notes and Re-View

5. Clockwork

This is a fun way to mix up groups, find connections, and move around a bit.

1. Make a list of qualities or descriptions that will guide the movements.

   Sample List
   - Only child
   - Have/had a family pet
   - A cat person
   - A dog person
   - Lived out of state for more than a year
   - Had perfect school attendance
   - Can run more than five miles at one time
   - Climbed a mountain
   - Been to a movie in the last week
   - Have brothers or sisters
   - Don't like chocolate
   - Been to a tropical island

2. On a large field or activity room floor, lay out 12 circles of rope, webbing, or cord on the ground in a clock-like pattern. The size of the circles depends on the size of the group. If there are 60 people in the group, there should be room for 8-10 people to stand with one foot in the circle. If the group has 100 people, there should be room for 12-15 people to stand in the circle.
3. When the group arrives, ask them to stand in the circles based on their birthdays. The one o'clock position is January, two o'clock is February, and so on.
4. Have them introduce themselves to the other people in their circles.
5. Get the group's attention and give a description or a quality and a direction for movement. For example, "If you're an only child, move three spaces clockwise when I say go. Go!"
6. Once the people who fit the description move the proper number of spaces, have them introduce themselves to the people in the new circle.
7. Get their attention again and repeat the process: "If your family had a pet while you were growing up, move six spaces counter-clockwise when I say go. Go!"
8. Repeat this until you run out of questions or just before they're tired of the activity.[154]

[154] "Kill it before it dies" is a very helpful concept for leading activities.

Equipment

You'll need 12 lengths of rope, webbing, or cord tied into circles. Hula hoops can be used for groups of up to 40-50. Creating a list of descriptions before the activity is very helpful as well.

Consider This

This activity can help you get an idea of who's in the group. Make your own list of items that relates to the topic you're teaching or an issue you'd like to address. Notice who moves each time and who doesn't. Encourage members of the group to observe who moves when they do and who doesn't, just so they can make some connections later on. You can also suggest that they think of some questions they'd like to ask those people who moved when they didn't. After the activity ends, encourage a time of interaction regarding any similarities and differences.

Variations

You can use this activity to create groups for other activities or to mix up groups that have been working together.

Personal Notes and Re-View

6. Circle in a Circle

Try this activity if you want people to create connections with several other people in a large group—one person at a time.

1. Have the entire group get into pairs.
2. Offer two choices and have the pairs decide which one they'll be: one or two, red or green, Batman or Superman.
3. Challenge them to see how quickly the Ones can arrange themselves with all the other Ones in a large circle and facing in, while all the Twos form their own circle inside the Ones' circle and facing out—a circle in a circle.
4. Let them know they'll be meeting several different people during this activity. And they're to ask and answer four questions each time they meet a new person.
5. The four questions are:

    - What is the best movie or TV show you've ever seen?
    - Where is the most beautiful place you've ever been?
    - What is one thing you'd like to do before you die?
    - Name one person, alive or dead, you'd like to have dinner with.

6. Have them ask and answer the questions with the person they're standing across from right now. Allow four or five minutes for the new pairs to talk. Give them a 30-second warning.
7. When it's time to quit, get their attention and tell one of the circles, inside or outside, to move a specific number of people a certain direction: "Outside circle move 10 people to your left."
8. Now ask them to introduce themselves and do the four questions with the new person they're facing.
9. Repeat this several times by having the different circles move in different directions and different numbers of people each time. Be sure to give them time to talk, but cut it off before people get bored.

Equipment

No equipment is required, but you may want to have copies of the questions posted around the room for people to reference.

Consider This

Watch and listen to how the pairs interact. Ask the group to think about or discuss the challenges in this activity. Did they find certain people to be easier to talk with than others? Did they feel they were given too much or too little time to interact with each person? Did they notice any differences when they were interacting with the same gender versus someone of the opposite gender?

Variations

I encourage you to create your own questions that more accurately address the unique needs of whatever group you're working with.

Personal Notes and Re-View

7. First Impressions

This is a fun way to practice meeting people for the first time and to play with first impressions.

1. Introduce this activity by reminding people they only have one chance to make a first impression. How they greet people and how they shake hands are two big factors in forming first impressions. A firm, confident handshake as they introduce themselves; making eye contact; and an interesting, intelligent opening question or remark go a long way to creating positive first impressions.
2. Let the group know that in a few minutes they'll be practicing first impressions on each other. They'll be asked to find one person, introduce themselves as they shake hands, and ask one good question. They'll have three minutes during each round to ask and answer each other's questions. After three minutes, they'll hear a signal to move on to another person and repeat the process.
3. Give them a minute to think of two or three good opening questions.
4. Sound the signal and start the activity.
5. Be sure to do at least four or five rounds so people get a chance to try a few different ways of creating first impressions.

Equipment

Nothing is needed for this activity.

Consider This

Watch and listen to how the pairs interact. Ask the group to think about or discuss the challenges in this activity. Did they find certain people easier to talk with than others? Did they feel they were given too much or too little time to interact with each person? Did they notice any differences when they were interacting with the same gender versus someone of the opposite gender?

Variations

A fun way to turn this into a role-play activity is to assign different impressions for the participants to give as they introduce themselves: confident, terrified, joyful, shy, pessimistic, and so on. With smaller groups, you can do this and then see if the person's partner can correctly identify the impression they were trying to make.

Personal Notes and Re-View

8. Tom's Two-Minute Frenzy

Tom Leahy[155] uses this simple, quick energizer to create connections and energy.

1. At the beginning of the event, training, or workshop, inform the group of what a two-minute frenzy entails.
2. When you announce, "TWO-MINUTE FRENZY! 15 people!" they'll have two minutes to introduce themselves to 15 different people.
3. Have them do a practice frenzy, just to get the hang of it.
4. Then several times throughout the event, announce a frenzy: "TWO-MINUTE FRENZY! 18 people!"

[155] A trainer, facilitator, builder, and overall extraordinary person, Tom offers amazing training programs for experiential professionals. He also hosts the best conference, which I attend every year: the National Challenge Course Practitioners Symposium (NCCPS). Check out www.Leahy-inc.com.

Equipment

Nothing is needed for this activity.

Personal Notes and Re-View

9. Building Community (individuals, small group, large group)

This activity takes advantage of the dynamics created by different sizes of groups. Plan on spending a few hours with this one.

1. Gather three different kinds of craft resources: 30 pipe cleaners, one box of paper clips and 100 3x5 cards (these go together in a bag), 50 "craft sticks,"[156] 50 soda straws, and so on. Be sure there are enough materials so each person can have enough of one resource to construct something.
2. As participants arrive for the activity, give them a brown paper bag containing one type of resource (craft item).
3. You may want to do a large group warm-up activity first. Then tell the group they'll be exploring "community" for the next few hours. Their brown paper bags contain their resources for building community.
4. Their first task is to find two other people who have different resources than they do. In other words, they should form a group with three different types of resource items represented. For example, one has craft sticks, another has pipe cleaners, and the third has straws.
5. Once they're in groups of three, let them know this first activity will be an individual event. They'll have 15 minutes to work on their own. As individuals, they must create something that represents community to them using all the resources found in their own paper bags. They must work alone and cannot borrow or use any other resources than those found in their own bags. They cannot use any symbols or letters found on a keyboard in their creations either.
6. Tell them to begin. Give them a two-minute warning and a 30-second warning to finish up their creations. Then after 15 minutes, tell them to stop.
7. Give them two minutes each to explain their creations to the other two people in their triads.
8. Once everyone has had a chance to share what they built with their groups of three, get the large group's attention and give them the next part of this activity.
9. They now have to build something that represents community to the groups of three. They must use all three resources in making their creations. They have 15 minutes to complete this task.
10. Be sure to give them two-minute and 30-second warnings before the end of the 15 minutes. When the time is up have them stop building.
11. This is a good time for a break. Invite them to leave their creations and check out the other groups' perspectives on community as they take a 10-minute break.
12. After the break, gather all the groups of three together and ask them to find two other groups of three to form a small group of nine.
13. Once they're in groups of nine, offer the next part of the challenge. As a group of nine, they must create something that represents community to all of them and also uses all the resources of all nine members of the group. They have 30 minutes to complete the project.

[156] I've always called these "Popsicle sticks," but I find them for much cheaper prices in craft stores labeled as "craft sticks."

14. At the end of the 30 minutes, give the groups an opportunity to present and explain their creations to the other groups.[157]
15. Gather all the small groups together after they've had a chance to present their creations to each other. The last challenge is for the entire group to use ALL the resources to create something that represents community. They have 30 minutes to complete the project.
16. After 30 minutes, have them stop working on the project and give them an opportunity to explain their creation to the facilitator(s).

[157] Depending on the size of the large group, you may want to have them present to just one or two other groups instead.

Equipment

You'll need brown paper bags, one for each participant, and lots of craft supplies. I suggest giving one-third of the participants 20 pipe cleaners each, another third 50 craft sticks each, and another third a box of paper clips and 100 3x5 cards each. Feel free to substitute other resources for the ones I've listed.

Consider This

One important thing to listen for is how each person understands community. Once they break into triads and small groups, how do they determine a group perspective of community? Just as important as what they decide and what they build is how they go about doing it. What do they do with the already created structures? Do they combine them? Do they use one as the base and deconstruct the others? Or do they tear them all down and start over? In the large group setting, how do they organize themselves? Do they take time to identify the talents and abilities of the different group members?

Variations

The items or resources you give to the participants can impact how they interact and how they think about community. Use items that are familiar to your group or items that are totally alien to them. Of course, you can also use things that are easily available or affordable to make this fit your budget.

Personal Notes and Re-View

PLANNING/ASSESSING EXERCISES

(5 OF THEM)

Chapter 2.4

The activities that follow are designed for youth leaders and teachers to use either while planning events and activities or while assessing what actions or insights might be helpful to an individual. (Note: These planning exercises tend to be fairly specific; therefore, they won't always lend themselves to "Variations" or, in some cases, a "Consider This" section.)

No single exercise is a cure-all, and no assessment will give you the whole story. These activities are useful tools, but they're no substitute for compassionate observation. You do this stuff until you create a real connection with your students and no longer need activities, exercises, or programs to interact with them.[158] The planning activities are the same way—they create an external structure that's only useful until you find an internal structure that works well for you.

Whether you use these activities as they're written or modify them to fit your unique situation, I hope you'll find them useful—not only for planning and assessing, but also in helping you find your own structure and voice as you help students learn and grow.[159]

1. Pressure Grid[160]

If you're working with someone[161] who is overly stressed or not stressed enough[162] this exercise creates a visual reference to how you're spending your time and how you might move things around to change your level of stress.

1. Make copies of the **Pressure Grid** handout **(page 115)** for each person.
2. Distribute the handout and ask the group to take 10-20 minutes to think about their activities from the past week. In the space provided, they should write down what they did and approximately how much time they spent doing each activity. For example, homework (eight hours), guitar lessons (three hours), TV (10 hours), and so on.
3. Now ask them to look at the pressure grid. It has two arrows that create four areas. One arrow represents pressure—how urgent or pressing something is. The

[158] "Technique is what teachers use until the real teacher arrives." —Parker Palmer in *Courage to Teach.*

[159] I would love to hear how you've used these exercises and activities. (BearLosey@sbcglobal.net)

[160] This grid is adapted from Stephen Covey's and the Franklin Covey workshops. Hopefully this version can be helpful for those of us who struggle with the fear of becoming a slave to a calendar or *PDA.*

[161] Including yourself.

[162] Stress can motivate you to get important things done. Stress gets us to turn off the TV or video game and out making a difference in the world. Both too much stress and too little stress are symptoms of not using your time and resources well.

other arrow represents significance—the importance or worth of an activity. The top-left area is for things that are pressing but not significant. This is "Stolen Time" and includes things like "must watch TV" and being at the donut shop when the fresh "old fashioneds" come out of the oven.

The top-right area represents activities that are both pressing and significant. These things are called "Actionable." Things in this area might include studying for a test that's scheduled for the next day or getting to work.

Things that aren't very pressing or significant belong in the bottom-left area. This is called "Wasted Time." Watching four hours of a ***SpongeBob SquarePants*** marathon or spending the same amount of time playing video games would fall into this area.

The last section, the bottom right, is for activities that aren't pressing but are significant. This area is called "Reflection/Planning" and includes things like journaling, creating a budget or to-do list, and organizing your desk.

4. Ask the participants to place each of the activities they've listed into one of the four areas. Remind them to be honest with themselves as they do this.[163]
5. After all the activities of the past week have been placed into one of the four areas, ask the group members to take some time to reflect and talk about what they noticed as they worked on the grid.
6. Now ask them to make a schedule for the next week, based on what they noticed from the pressure grid.

[163] Combat video games aren't considered "job training" unless you're going to be a soldier.

Equipment

Copies of the **Pressure Grid** handout **(page 115)** and something to write with for each person.

Consider This

The point of this activity is to get you to notice how you use your time. Spending time in the "Stolen" or "Wasted" areas may not be the best plan. Time spent there tends to increase your stress level by forcing more things into the "actionable" area or just not getting things done. If you find yourself living in the "Actionable" area your stress level is probably through the roof.[164] Most people don't spend enough time in "Reflection/Planning." This is where you can sort out what needs to get done and when. The surprising thing is that you also will find more time to do the fun things that would normally get pressed out due to stolen or wasted time.[165]

[164] You probably also prioritize horizontally—everything is important and must get done *right now*.

[165] www.Praxistraining.com offers workshops and coaching for people who don't like calendars and schedules, but still want to reduce their stress and get the right stuff done.

Personal Notes and Re-View

Pressure Grid

Why are you stressed? How can you get more of the right stuff done? This worksheet may give you some ideas about how to reduce your stress and get on to doing the right stuff in your life.

Take 10-20 minutes to reflect on the past week. Think about all the things you've done. (You can use your calendar, if you keep one, to help you remember.) In the box below, list everything you've done this past week and approximately how much time you spent doing each thing.

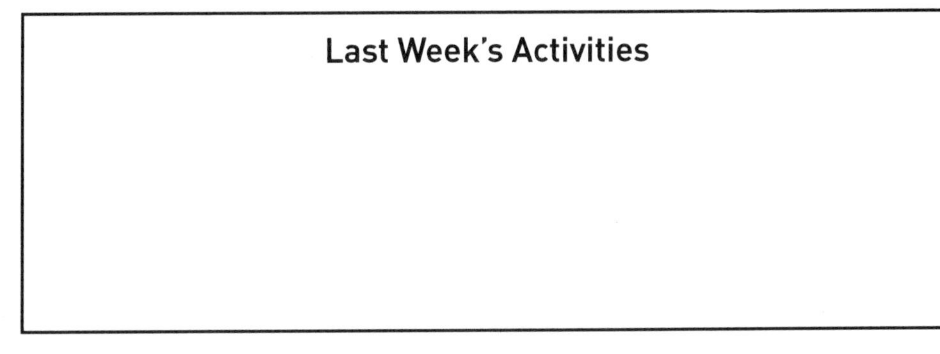

Now place each of the activities listed above into one of the four areas in the pressure grid below.

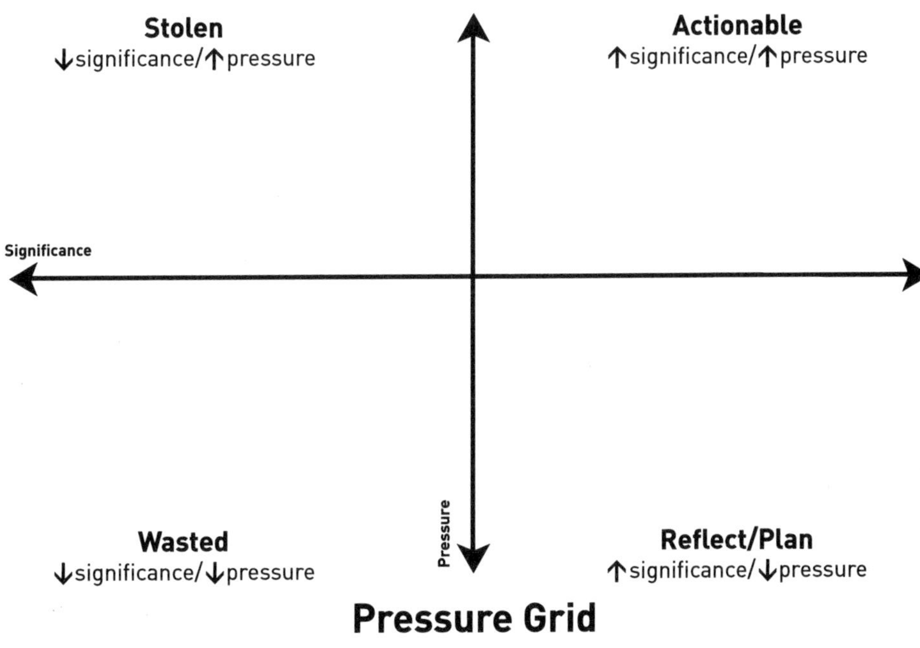

Pressure Grid

- What do you notice?
- Are you spending enough time in the Reflect/Plan area?
- How can you reduce the amount of time spent in the high-stress Actionable area?
- How much time do you typically spend in the Wasted or Stolen areas?

Take what you've learned from this Pressure Grid and make yourself a balanced schedule for next week.

2. The Organizational Chart

If you're working with a new group of people or want to better understand a student clique, this exercise (adapted from the world of field anthropology) will tell you a lot about the individuals in the group and also about the group itself.

1. Gather the group around a table with some flip chart paper and pens. Ask them if there are groups or cliques at their school. Have them list all the different groups they can think of. If they don't do so on their own, remind them that the teachers, administrators, and staff are part of the school too.
2. Once they have a list of groups, ask them to create an organizational chart for their school using these groups. Before they start, you may want to give them an idea of what is meant by an "organizational chart" (or "org. chart"). It's like a map of how the different groups relate to each other—which groups share members and which groups don't? Who has influence and power and who doesn't? How well do the different groups get along? Have them draw symbols that represent each group and then create different symbols to represent how the groups relate to each other.
3. You may want to show them a few different examples of org. charts not only to give them an idea of how they work, but also to give them the freedom to create new shapes, symbols, and relationships.
4. If you have several groups working at the same time, you can give them time at the end of the activity to present their org. charts to the other groups.

Equipment

You'll need several pieces of flip chart paper or poster paper and a set of colored pens for each group.

Consider This

Listen to the group's discussion, which will be just as important as the chart they create. Are the groups easily identified? Which ones are more difficult than others? How do they decide on the names of the different groups? Which groups are represented by people sitting at the table? Which groups are not? What symbols do they create for each group? The size of the symbol will tell you something about what they think of the group it represents; the larger and more complex the symbol, the more important or powerful they think the group is. Placement on the page is important as well; center or top placement tends to show more significance than a bottom location or out toward the edges of the paper.

Variations

Another version of this activity is to have them draw a detailed map of their school and where each group hangs out. Size and proportions will tell you a lot about what they feel is important.

Personal Notes and Re-View

3. Comfort Zone/Wellness Target

Try this activity if you'd like a group to understand how different they are and still get to know each other at a deeper level. (You'll need to review where I shared about Comfort Zones [see Section One: Dynamics of Growth] and Wellness [see Section One: Spheres of Growth] before you lead this activity.)

1. Set up tables with no more than eight chairs, some flip chart paper (two or three sheets), and several pens.
2. Create a list of 10 to 15 scenarios that may challenge people in different areas of the Wellness Wheel.
3. Have the group gather around the tables in teams of eight.
4. Briefly explain Comfort Zone Theory and have them draw a large diagram that includes the different comfort zones.
5. Briefly explain the Wellness Wheel and have them draw the different areas on the same paper and in the same circle as the comfort zones (figure 18).
6. Present a series of scenarios and ask them to write their initials in the area and level of comfort where they'd find themselves for each one.
7. Be sure to stop and discuss what they notice after every two or three scenarios.

Possible Scenarios:

- A physics exam
- Asking a single person of the opposite sex for his or her phone number
- Going to the movies alone
- Doing 100 push-ups
- Eating sushi
- Praying
- Presenting a spiritual message to a group of 500 people
- Planning a party
- Admitting you can't do something
- Crying in front of strangers
- Leading a group of 50 in worship
- Going on a 10-day backpacking trip with a group of strangers
- Sharing your faith and beliefs with someone you know doesn't agree with you
- Writing and performing an original song for your family
- Sharing your most painful emotional experience with a new friend
- Shaving your head
- Being shipwrecked on a deserted island with a strict Buddhist
- Running a 10K race
- Painting a picture that will be displayed at your school

Figure 18
Comfort Zone/Wellness Target

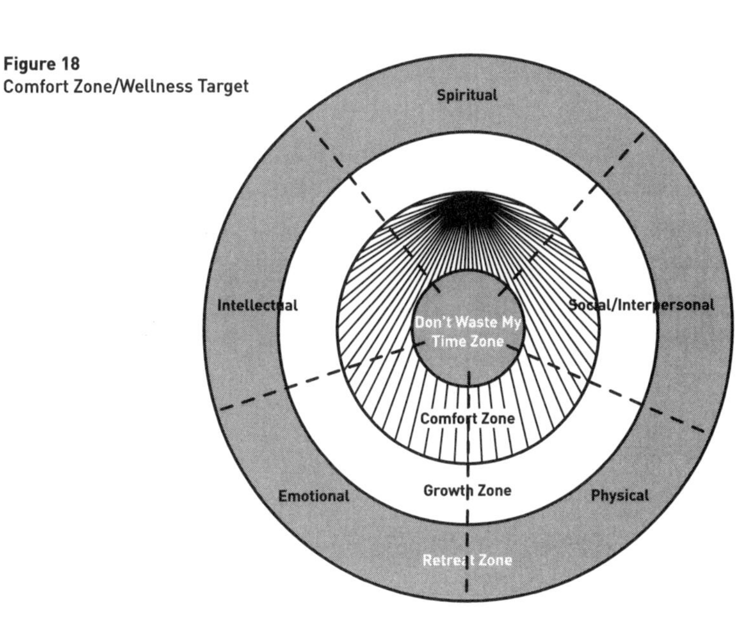

Equipment

You'll need to have enough flip chart or poster paper for each table to create a diagram. You'll also need pens to draw the diagram and for the group to record where they'd place themselves in each scenario. There are several books that contain more scenarios like the ones in this sample list. They'd make great resources for this activity.[166]

[166] *Would You Rather...? 465 Provocative Questions to Get Teenagers Talking* by Doug Fields (YS/Zondervan, 1996) and *Have You Ever...? 450 Intriguing Questions to Get Teenagers Talking* by Les Christie (YS/Zondervan, 1998).

Safety

The depth and quality of this activity depends on how safe the group feels emotionally and interpersonally. If you're using it as a "get to know you" activity, don't expect earth-shattering revelations. If the group has been together for a while and some trust has been built, this activity could be a huge step toward deeper and more compassionate interactions.

Consider This

Ask the group to consider carefully areas of Wellness and Comfort Zone Theory—particularly which comfort zone they'd be in for each scenario. Why might different people be in different comfort zones for the same situation? Why might they place themselves in different spots on the Wellness Wheel for the same activity? What are the implications for being part of a group?

Personal Notes and Re-View

4. Breakdown Components/Sequenced Learning Planner

1. This system will help you break lessons into parts so you can easily create a sequenced learning opportunity.[167]

2. Select a lesson topic. This can be a concept like faith or forgiveness, a skill like Bible study or building, or even lessons in other areas like writing or chemistry. Be sure the topic you choose is "bite-sized"—large enough to be interesting, but not so large that it can't be covered in the time you have.

3. What are the different parts of that topic? Take 15-20 minutes to brainstorm all the component concepts that make up the lesson. Take the first 5-10 minutes to write down everything that pops into your mind. Use the rest of the time to consult resources to fill in what you may have missed.

4. Look at the list you created. Try to clearly define each part. Combine similar concepts and try to establish where one idea stops and another one starts. Some of this defining will be very natural, but you may have to draw some artificial lines to create useful concepts.

5. Look over your list of defined components to see if they're still clearly linked to the topic of your lesson. Is there any natural sequence, order, or priority that presents itself? Is there any concept of *component* that is fundamental to understanding other parts? Use a line drawing and letters to show connections and priorities.

6. On a fresh page, list the parts of the lesson in a sequence that starts simple and moves toward more complexity. Does this sequence create a step-by-step process that leads to the goal of the lesson? Did it create any confusion or side issues that may need to be addressed later?

7. Take a few minutes to come up with two or three simple ways you might present each component part and what resources you might need.

[167] See Section One: "Stages of Growth."

Equipment

You might want to use a copy of the **Sequenced Learning Planner (page 121)**.

Personal Notes and Re-View

Sequenced Learning Planner

____

LESSON TOPIC

Breakdown

In the space below write down all the parts or components that make up the lesson topic. Don't worry about being correct at this point. Just list as many parts as possible.

Breakdown

Define and Prioritize

Clearly define in the box below the parts and concepts listed above. Combine similar ideas to create defined parts that make up the lesson topic. Look for natural connections, priorities, or sequences. Use lines, letters, or numbers to show these connections and priorities.

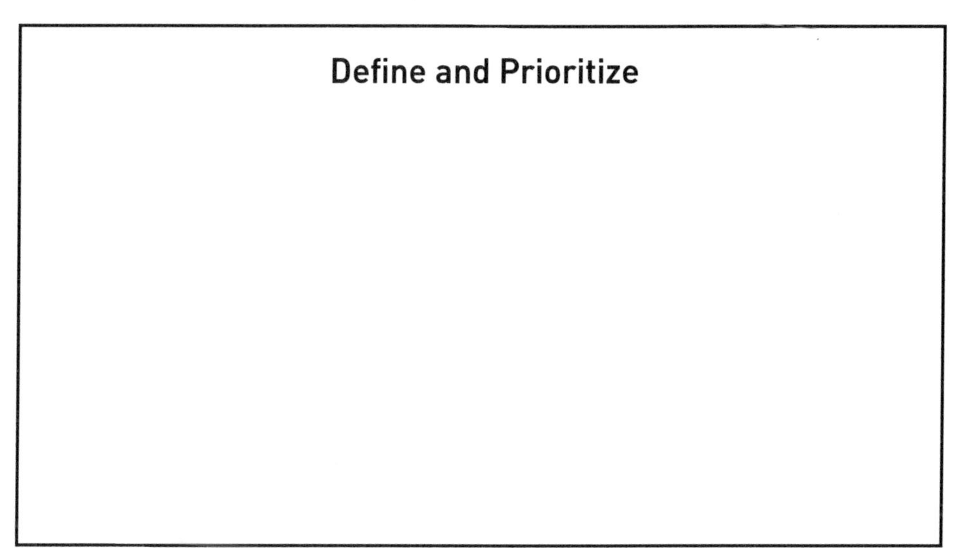

Sequence

Using the definitions and priorities from the previous section create a sequence of components or parts for your lesson. List two or three creative ideas for how you might present each part.

Sequenced Lesson Plan

1.
→
→
→

2.
→
→
→

3.
→
→
→

4.
→
→
→

5.
→
→
→

6.
→
→
→

7.
→
→
→

5. Jar of Death[168]

This activity takes advantage of performance anxiety to motivate people to complete or improve an assignment.

1. Create a list of five tasks for a person or group to complete. These tasks should be things they can prepare for and practice.[169]
2. Explain each task.
3. Show them the Jar of Death and let them know that each of these tasks has been written on a slip of paper and placed in the jar. They'll have 90 minutes[170] to prepare, then they'll be asked to take a slip of paper from the Jar of Death and perform that task.

[168] If "Jar of Death" seems a bit extreme, feel free to change the name. "Jar of Stress," "Container of Discomfort," and "The Icky Jar" are just a few of the many options to consider.

[169] See the *Sample Task Lists* in the Equipment section.

[170] The time will depend on the type of group and tasks to be completed. Allow 30-45 minutes if you assign Initiative Activities to groups. You may allow several days if you assign lesson-planning activities to teachers or leaders.

Equipment

You'll need some sort of container to act as the Jar of Death, a list of tasks or assignments for each person or group, and individual slips of paper (with the tasks written on them) to be placed into the Jar of Death.

Sample Task Lists

For Groups:

- Sing a song.
- Perform an original group chant.
- Using all the members of the group, create a working human sculpture of your group's favorite home appliance. You have two minutes to complete this task.
- Have your entire group stand only on a T-shirt for 30 seconds. The T-shirt is on the floor but the group cannot touch the floor. They can only touch the T-shirt or each other.
- Construct and deconstruct a human pyramid using all the members of the group in 30 seconds.
- Set up and take down a tent in three minutes.
- Do a group "lap-sit" and hold it for 15 seconds. You have three minutes to complete this task.

For Individuals and Staff:

Select tasks and skills related to their job descriptions or a topic you're teaching.

Variations

I use this activity in staff training events to create some urgency around learning job responsibilities and tasks. If they'll have to teach lessons, I'll give them a list of several different topics for them to create either lesson outlines or stories they'll have to perform. If there are skills or tasks associated with a job—such as setting up a sound system or chairs, or making posters—I include these in the Jar of Death as well.

Personal Notes and Re-View

ACTIVITIES AND EXERCISES INDEX

Chapter 2.5

Initiative Activities

Exercises for Small Groups

Large Group Activities

Planning/Assessing Exercises

Section Three

TEMPLATES—MODELS AND ACTIVITIES TOGETHER

TEMPLATES

MODELS AND ACTIVITIES TOGETHER

So what's a ***template*** anyway? Templates are patterns. They give you an idea of what something will look like when it's finished, and they offer direction and vision for something that may not be totally clear. They're not binding, and they're not the finished product. I've seen templates used as outlines to show you where to cut,[171] but you still choose what to cut and have to do the cutting. I've seen templates used to show where to place pieces and parts, but you still select the pieces and place the parts.

So far this book has offered pieces and parts. If you've never used experiential methods or led these types of activities before, you still may not have a clear idea about how this stuff works in common ministry situations.

Therefore, I offer these simple templates to you for vision and direction. You may be able to duplicate them exactly,[172] but more likely they'll give you a general idea of how the models and activities are applied. Then you should select the pieces that apply to your unique situation and place the parts that work best for you. These templates focus on using the models and activities found in this book. The emphasis is more on interactions and learning than on programming.[173] For example, how can we structure a community service project that helps students gain new life skills and perspectives, moves them out of their comfort zones, and helps integrate different aspects of their lives? Can we go on a short-term mission trip that throws our students into disequilibrium and helps them live differently back at home? What about real-life interactions with students? Can we take these unplanned moments and turn them into life-changing, teachable moments?

The templates that follow offer an idea on how to apply the experiential theories and models from the first section, using the activities and exercises from the second section. Models, when by themselves, are "mental gymnastics" that are fun to talk about. Activities can just be fun. But activities without models lack direction, and models without activities lack impact. When we intentionally use activities in the light of experiential methods and models, we create powerful learning situations. The templates are an offering and a challenge for you to intentionally create amazing interactions for you, your staff, and your students on your own.

171 Templates are used in woodworking as well as sewing. Both involve cutting.

172 I doubt it. The biggest mistake made after purchasing a book or going to a workshop is trying to apply the programs and ideas exactly as written or explained. You live and work in a unique context with a unique group of people. YOU'RE the expert when it comes to your context. I can offer advice and ideas, but you must do the work of adapting them to your situation.

173 The templates in my previous book on this topic, *The Experiential Youth Ministry Handbook*, focus primarily on programming.

COMMUNITY SERVICE

Chapter 3.1

Whether it's washing windows at the local senior center or cleaning bathrooms at local gas stations, community service projects aren't merely ways for your group to express Christ's love for the community. They can also be amazing opportunities for individual and group growth.

You'll need to be intentional about making your community service project a learning opportunity. What do you want your group to learn from this experience? There are many topics from which to choose: service, humility, social justice, love, compassion, and more. Don't try to cover everything in one event. You can do several community service projects each year and cover a different topic each time.

Select one topic to focus on for this first project. The topic and the project should work together to impact your students. Select a topic based on your service project, or select a project based on what you want your group to wrestle with. You should select your topic and project at least four months before the date of the event. This will give you plenty of time to set up the details[174] and allow the group to gain skills and perspectives they'll need while on the project. As soon as you've selected a topic, you should take some time to do the **Sequenced Learning Planner**[175] activity. The results of this activity will help you plan a series of lessons that will prepare your students to get the most they can from the service project.

There are several challenges you may encounter as you plan community service projects. One is selecting a project that will take the students out of their comfort zones yet not force them into the retreat zone. Picking up trash around the church is a wonderful thing, but it may not create a very powerful learning opportunity. Picking up trash on Skid Row at midnight is a wonderful thing as well, but it may be way into the retreat zone of many of your students.[176]

It's a good idea to get your students involved in the planning process. Before you decide what you're going to do for a service project, you can do a few activities with your students to find out what challenges them and how they see their community. The **Comfort Zone/Wellness Target**[177] activity is a great way to assess what project may put them into the growth zone without causing them to retreat. Make a list that includes several different project options, and then notice what area and what level of challenge they assign to each.

[174] There are two great exercises that deal with logistics in the "Planning Activities" section of my first book, *The Experiential Youth Ministry Handbook.*

[175] Planning/Assessing Exercise #4 (page 120).

[176] Not to mention their parents and their parents' lawyers.

[177] Planning/Assessing Exercise #3 (page 118).

Another activity that may be helpful in choosing a project is the **Organizational Chart**[178] exercise. Instead of having them chart their school, have them create an organizational chart of the community. After they've done that, have them create a map that shows the major parts of their community and where the different groups are found. Watch and listen to your students as they do this exercise. You'll notice people and locations that they feel would benefit from their service. You may even hear them mention project ideas as they create their charts and maps.

[178] Planning/Assessing Exercise #2 (page 116).

Working as a group while still dealing with individuals' comfort zone dynamics is another difficulty you face in doing community service projects. A few hours spent focusing on how a group works together can help you deal with this challenge. Several weeks before the event, you can have your group try the **Clips and Cards**[179] exercise. After they've built one card tower, talk about how they decided on a design and how they divided up the labor. Explore the importance of being involved and the creative ways to stay involved besides actually building the structure.[180] Be sure to discuss how building the card tower is related to the service project. If time permits, have them build a second tower that is taller than their first effort. The catch is they can only use the resources that were used when making the first tower. This will force them to face the challenge of getting more done with the same or fewer resources. (Two other activities that will emphasize the challenges you may face during a community service project are **Blindfolded Tent Building**[181] and **Leonardo's Bridge**.[182])

[179] Exercise for Small Groups #1 (page 85).

[180] Encouraging, gathering resources, caring for the builders, and so on.

[181] Initiative Activity #21 (page 79).

[182] Initiative Activity #20 (page 78).

As the project date approaches, give all the students (whether they'll be doing the project or not) a small journal and ask them to record their thoughts about the project and their involvement. Be sure to tell them to bring the journal to the event, if they're going. On the day of the event, encourage them to use the journal to write down their thoughts, feelings, and observations. Help them journal by creating several opportunities for them to write—as they arrive at the project site, an hour after they start the project, during a meal or break, before they get ready to leave the project.

On the day of the project, it will also be important that you give them a chance to debrief the experience. You may want to do this away from the actual project location—back at church, in a back room of a restaurant, or at someone's home. You'll want a location with limited distractions and some privacy so students feel comfortable sharing their authentic reactions to the day.

A good way to start the debriefing session is with the **"And Then...But Before That..."**[183] activity. This will get them talking and sharing their perspectives of the experience. Have them do this first without referencing their journals. Then have them look at their journals and see if they'd add anything or change the order of events. After they've had a chance to discuss and debrief the day, let them know that the next time they meet, they'll be sharing some of these perspectives with the group members who couldn't attend. Challenge them to think about how this experience might change how they see the world and how they live their lives. What will they do with the new perspectives they've gained from doing this project?

[183] Exercise for Small Groups #5 (page 90).

When it comes to learning and growth, the group meetings that follow the project are as important as the project itself. If they were tossed into disequilibrium by the project and were forced to gain new skills or perspectives, they'll need a chance to identify and practice these new insights. Be sure to allow for at least one group follow-up lesson and create one-on-one opportunities for individuals to process their lessons in private too.

Community service projects offer real-life experiences that lead students out of their comfort zones in order to gain new and powerful insights. These experiences will challenge students to learn how they can be Christ to their neighbors and how they can show compassion and love to their communities. The more intentional you are as a leader, the more powerful and practical the project becomes.

SHORT-TERM MISSIONS

Chapter 3.2

When planning a short-term mission trip, it's important to remember that the impact will be far greater on your students than on the people you're going to work with and for.[184] With the intentional use of the experiential methods and activities in this book, you can squeeze every drop of impact from the experience. At their best, short-term mission trips benefit everyone involved. The people you serve benefit from your energy and resources, and your students come home with powerful insights that impact your community.

[184] Most of the short-term mission organizations I've worked with state this in their materials. This is not intended to diminish the benefit of the work you'll do, but to emphasize the potential impact on the group that does the serving.

I encourage you to use one of the many great short-term mission organizations to help you plan your trip. They have connections in the local community, know who will benefit most from your efforts, and can usually access resources and materials easily and inexpensively. They have worked out the logistics already, and they can save you a lot of time, energy, and money.[185] These organizations take much of the logistical burden off you so you'll have the time and energy to focus on your students' learning and growth.

[185] Groups like Amor Ministries, Genesis Expeditions, YWAM, and others can help you decide where, how, and when your group can experience a short-term mission.

Once you've decided you'd like your students to experience a short-term mission, you want to start planning right away. While many organizations can accommodate last-minute sign-ups, if you wait too long, you'll add tons of stress to yourself, your students, and the organization, and you won't be able to take full advantage of all the learning and growth this type of experience has to offer. If you choose to go with an existing short-term mission organization, you should contact them at least six months before you want to go.[186] If you're really organized, you can contact them nine months or more ahead of time and have plenty of space to do fundraising, gather resources, and intentionally use experiential methods to increase the learning opportunities for your students.

[186] If you want to plan your own trip, you should start planning much earlier.

Beyond the logistics of going on a short-term mission trip, you'll want to be intentional about what you want your students to learn from the experience. The **Sequenced Learning Planner**[187] can help you not only identify the learning and skills this trip will demand of your students, but it will also help you design a series of lessons that will help the students gain them as well. Do this activity to help you lay out a general plan for lessons and activities leading up to the trip. Do this activity again for the individual lessons identified. Topics such as cultural differences,

[187] Planning/Assessing Exercise #4 (page 120).

servant leadership, and compassion are important topics for any trip. Other topics will depend on the type of mission trip and project you choose.

If you're doing a building project, you may want to offer some skill-building activities around the materials and tools you'll be using. If your project involves teaching or leading activities, you may want to offer training in these areas. Once you've identified key lessons and skills and offered some training and experience in those areas, the **Jar of Death**[188] activity can be a fun way to see just how ready they are to go on the trip. As you start the training, let the students know that the key skills will be placed in the Jar of Death and you'll do the activity during the last training session before you leave on the trip.

[188] Planning/Assessing Exercise #5 (page 123).

The **Comfort Zone/Wellness Target**[189] activity is a great way to assess where students will be most challenged, and it can also help you identify topics you can address before you leave. Create a list of scenarios that include situations they'll probably face: sleeping in a tent with five other people, not being able to take a shower for three days, telling a Bible story to people who speak a different language, mixing and pouring cement, and so on. Notice where they place these activities in the target and listen to the conversations as they do this activity. You'll discover where individuals will be challenged, and you'll discover who is most comfortable with each situation. This can give you insight into assigning students to teams and tasks.

[189] Planning/Assessing Exercise #3 (page 118).

Traveling and living in close quarters can be more challenging than the actual project. Creating a series of increasingly challenging team-building experiences can set up more significant interactions while you're on the trip.[190] You can have the group do an initiative activity at the start or end of each trip meeting or training time. Start with something simple[191] such as **Collection of Knots**[192] or **Bucket Lift**.[193] These activities will get the group working together. As the departure date gets closer, you can increase the complexity of the challenges by doing activities such as **Toxic Waste**[194] and **Proton Transfer**.[195] It's worthwhile to include money in your fundraising for a trip to a challenge course. There you can have a trained facilitator lead your students through initiatives and high-challenge activities. Not only will this build a strong team that works together well, but it will also increase the confidence level of the individual students. They'll experience success as a group and see that they can handle far more than they think they can as individuals.

[190] See Section One "Stages of Growth."

[191] Here the word *simple* means "straightforward." It does not mean "easy."

[192] Initiative Activity #13 (page 68).

[193] Initiative Activity #1 (page 51).

[194] Initiative Activity #12 (page 67).

[195] Initiative Activity #4 (page 56).

The learning starts as soon as they sign up for the trip. Create an information packet that not only includes the logistical details, but also outlines what they might experience and how they might learn and grow. Create a trip journal that has pages for pretrip assignments, observations while on the trip, and post-trip reflection. Use these journals intentionally by creating open space in your trip meetings and training sessions for them to write. Wrap up meetings with provocative questions for them to ponder and journal about on their own time. While on the trip, encourage the students to spend a few minutes each day recording their experiences and how they're reacting in the moment. After the trip is over, these journals become wonderful discussion starters for follow-up meetings. They also create a physical reminder of the lessons they learned and the changes they made as a result of the mission trip.

The students will need opportunities for rest and reflection both during and after the trip.[196] These moments free up space and energy for them to start to identify

[196] See Comfort Zone Theory in Section One: "Dynamics of Growth."

and grasp the powerful lessons they're learning. If they don't have any down time or play time, they won't be able to connect with many of the teachable moments they encounter. These moments can be formal discussions or informal conversations around the campfire or dinner table.[197] After you get home from the trip, these discussions are just as important. At least one post-trip meeting should focus on the specific lessons and observations the students brought home and specific plans on how they can apply them in their own communities and homes. Some of these lessons and plans may result in the students' desire to do service projects in their own communities.[198]

[197] Don't confuse these debrief/discussion sessions with Bible studies or seminars. These are opportunities for the students to express what they've experienced and are learning, not for you to tell them what they ought to be learning.

[198] See the previous section for a template on community service projects.

REAL-LIFE INTERVENTIONS

Chapter 3.3

The most powerful lessons I've learned and taught didn't come from a planned lesson or a programmed moment. They were "teachable moments"—instances where real life offered up an opportunity for growth that could be noticed and pointed out, where there was an invitation to grab it, and encouragement to play. These are the real-life interventions that result in dynamic, individualized learning. These are the opportunities that can be squandered if we don't notice them or have the insight to take advantage of them.

The models offered in Section One of this book offer a structure to help you notice and point out growth opportunities to the students and staff you work with. Even a basic understanding of the **Stages of Growth** can provide insight into a student's dilemma. The concept of **Disequilibrium** creates a structure for you to offer the appropriate comfort or support for a stressed-out staff member. The **Wellness Wheel** offers a way of understanding and communicating with a parent who's going through a divorce and wondering why her child's grades are dropping.

If you didn't really grasp the models in the first part of this book,[199] take some time to look over them again. Wrestle with them and dive deeper into the models that make the most sense to you. You may be intuitive and be able to sense when a student is approaching you with a significant issue. These models can clarify that intuition and suggest some options for you to offer the student.

Because individual interventions are unique by definition, it's difficult to create a useful template other than gaining a deeper understanding of how people learn and grow. I can offer two exercises you can do with students that may help identify what is stressing them out and where they may be able to ask for help.

Many students are overcommitted or don't have the personal discipline to handle the commitments they have. **The Pressure Grid**[200] activity helps students see for themselves where they may be losing time and energy. As they look at where they spend their time, they can see where their choices increase their stress levels. They can also use these insights to make better choices. If a student who approaches you seems to be overwhelmed by life, have her complete the Pressure Grid and create a simple schedule for the next week. Then meet with her again and have her redo the

[199] You may not fully grasp these ideas either because they may be brand new to you or because you skipped the first part of this book and went straight to the games and templates.

[200] Planning/Assessing Exercise #1 (page 113).

Pressure Grid. As she makes better choices, her stress levels will go down. She'll realize that the choices she makes can impact the quality of her day.[201, 202]

The **Comfort Zone/Wellness Target**[203] offers a way to focus a conversation with a struggling student. Grab one of these worksheets or just draw the target diagram on a napkin. Briefly explain the different zones and areas, then have him start to talk about what's going on in his life. When he mentions a significant event or a part of his life, have him write it down in the zone and area where he thinks it fits best. Ask questions that will encourage him to explore different areas of his life—areas of success and comfort, along with areas of challenge and failure.

Notice where different events and situations are placed, but also notice how the student describes them and talks about them. As you listen and observe try to identify the issues that the student will need to deal with the challenge on his own. Also identify those issues where you can offer support and encouragement. You may not be able to solve the upcoming divorce of his parents, but you can help him with his homework or drive him to practice. Sometimes just clearing away the clutter and identifying the real challenges can go a long way to helping a student succeed.

These are two exercises that can help guide an interaction when you notice the potential for teachable moments. They don't apply to every situation or every person, but the more models and theories you have in your bag[204] the more likely you'll have some sort of structure to work with in a teachable moment. The models and theories I cover in this book just scratch the surface of what's out there. I challenge you to dive deeper into these models and go hunting for others that you may find more useful.

[201] "How we spend our days is, of course, how we spend our lives." —Anne Dillard

[202] I realize this exercise is not the golden bullet that will solve all the problems of an overwhelmed kid. It's just a starting point that may lead to other insights that can be noticed and addressed.

[203] Planning/Assessing Exercise #3 (page 118).

[204] Just as you might have a bag of tricks for activities and recreation, I challenge you to collect a bag of models that you can call on when working with people.

APPENDIX

Going Deeper
(A Bibliography of Suggested Resources, Training, and Reading)

Books to Check Out

Anderson, Mike, Jim Cain, Chris Cavert, and Tom Heck. ***Teambuilding Puzzles***. Flagstaff, AZ: FUNdoing Publications, 2005.

Becker, Ernest. ***The Denial of Death***. New York: Simon & Schuster, 1973.

Bridges, William. ***Transitions: Making Sense of Life's Changes***. Reading, MA: Addison-Wesley, 1980.

Buber, Martin. ***I and Thou***. New York: Charles Scribner's Sons, 1970.

Cavert, Chris. ***The Possibles Bag***. Flagstaff, AZ: FUNdoing Publications, 2003.[205]

———, and Sam Sikes. ***50 Ways to Use Your Noodle: Loads of Land Games with Foam Noodle Toys***. Tulsa, OK: Learning Unlimited Corp., 1997.

Cain, Jim, and Barry Jolliff. ***Teamwork & Teamplay***. Dubuque, IA: Kendall/Hunt, 1998.[206]

Covey, Stephen R. ***The 7 Habits of Highly Effective People***. New York: Simon & Schuster, Fireside, 1989.

Fowler, James W. ***Becoming Adult, Becoming Christian: Adult Development and Christian Faith***. New York: Harper & Row, 1984.

———. ***Faith Development and Pastoral Care***. Edited by Don S. Browning. Philadelphia, PA: Fortress Press, 1987.

Freire, Paulo. ***Pedagogy of the Oppressed***. Translated by Myra Bergman Ramos. New York: Continuum International Publishing Group, 1993.

[205] This is a backpack that Chris Cavert offers from FUNdoing. It also comes with an activities book by the same name.

[206] This book has an extremely thorough resource section. It lists hundreds of books, articles, conferences, and organizations that focus on experiential education. I highly recommend getting this book!

Gilligan, Carol. ***In a Different Voice: Psychological Theory and Women's Development.*** Cambridge, MA: Harvard University Press, 1982.

Hamachek, Don E. ***Encounters With the Self.*** 3rd ed. New York: Holt, Rinehart and Winston, 1987.

Johnson, Kevin. ***Mission Trip Prep Kit: Leader's Guide.*** Grand Rapids, MI: YS/Zondervan, 2003.

Lamott, Anne. ***Bird by Bird: Some Instructions on Writing and Life.*** New York: Random House, Anchor Books, 1994.

Loder, James E. ***The Transforming Moment.*** 2nd ed. Colorado Springs, CO: Helmers and Howard, 1989.

Losey, John. ***The Experiential Youth Ministry Handbook.*** Grand Rapids, MI: YS/Zondervan, 2004.

Merton, Thomas. ***No Man Is an Island.*** New York: Harcourt Brace, 1955.

Nouwen, Henri J. M. ***Reaching Out.*** Grand Rapids, MI: Zondervan, 1998.

———. ***Life of the Beloved: Spiritual Living in a Secular World.*** New York: The Crossroad Publishing Co., 1992.

Palmer, Parker J. ***The Courage to Teach.*** San Francisco: Jossey-Bass, 1998.

———. ***To Know as We Are Known: A Spirituality of Education.*** San Francisco: Harper & Row, 1983.

Peck, M. Scott. ***The Different Drum: Community Making and Peace.*** New York: Simon & Schuster, 1987.

Perry, William G. Jr. ***Forms of Intellectual and Ethical Development in the College Years.*** New York: Holt, Rinehart and Winston, 1970.

Pink, Daniel H. ***A Whole New Mind: Moving from the Information Age to the Conceptual Age.*** New York: The Penguin Group, 2005.

Postman, Neil. ***Amusing Ourselves to Death: Public Discourse in the Age of Show Business.*** New York: Viking Penguin Inc., 1985.

———. ***The Disappearance of Childhood.*** New York: Delacorte Press, 1982.

Rohnke, Karl. ***The Bottomless Bag***. Dubuque, IA: Kendall/Hunt, 1991.

———. ***Cowstails and Cobras II: A Guide to Games, Initiatives, Ropes Courses & Adventure Curriculum***. Dubuque, IA: Kendall/Hunt, 1989.

———. ***Silver Bullets: A Guide to Initiative Problems, Adventure Games and Trust Activities***. Dubuque, IA: Kendall/Hunt, 1984.

Schotz, Amiel. ***Theatre Games and Beyond***. Colorado Springs, CO: Meriwether Publishing, 1998.

Web Sites to Visit

www.DoingWorks.com—Sam Sikes' site, which offers experience-based training and books.

www.Fundoing.com—Chris Cavert's site contains great resources and books for teachers, trainers, and other leaders.

www.FunStuffusa.com—***The*** place to get huge amounts of Silly Putty.

www.Leahy-inc.com—Tom Leahy's site contains information about challenge course construction and facilitation training.

www.LoseyExperience.blogspot.com—John Losey's blog on experiential methods.

www.Praxistraining.com—John Losey's site contains information about experience-based ministry, consulting, and training.

www.Teamworkandteamplay.com—Jim Cain's site contains information about team training and team-building equipment and books.

Conferences to Attend

The Core—"[Youth Specialties'] premiere one-day training event for your youth ministry. Every spring [the CORE] visit[s] over 100 cities across the U.S. and Canada, so chances are [they'll] visit a city near you! You and your volunteer team will benefit from this affordable, local training as you learn practical, beneficial realities, values, and skills for youth ministry." For more information, go to http://core.go.youthspecialties.com.

Emergent Events—"Emergent Village is a growing, generative friendship among missional Christians seeking to love our world in the Spirit of Jesus Christ." For more information, check out www.emergentvillage.us/.

National Challenge Course Practitioners Symposium (NCCPS)—held annually in Boulder, Colorado, and hosted by Tom Leahy. Go to www.Leahy-inc.com and click on the NCCPS link for more information.

National Youth Workers Convention—Youth Specialties' annual conference that's offered in three or four locations around the United States each fall. See www.youthspecialties.com for future dates and information.